WINDOWS ON·THE·WORLD

TRAINS *and* RAILWAYS

Written by
Sydney Wood

Illustrated by
Sergio

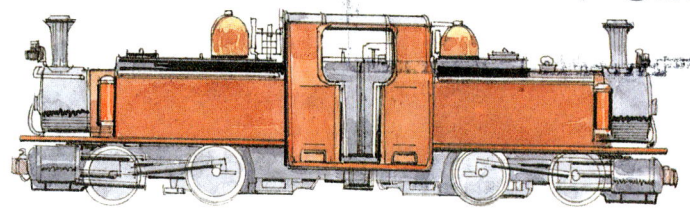

DORLING KINDERSLEY · LONDON

CONTENTS

4	A TRANSPORT REVOLUTION
6	THE FIRST TRAINS
8	THE AGE OF STEAM
10	MEN AT WORK
12	A CHANGE OF GAUGE
14	THE PEOPLE TRAVEL
16	HEADING WEST
18	UNDER ATTACK
20	COAST TO COAST
24	THE CIRCUS IS COMING
26	HEAVY WORK
28	STRANGE TRAINS
30	THE AGE OF ROMANCE
34	A POWER RACE
36	LAST GASP
38	UP FRONT
40	THE TRAIN NOW STANDING...
42	EN ROUTE
46	CITY TRAVEL
48	GOING UNDERGROUND
50	TUNNELS AND TUNNELLING
52	OVERCOMING OBSTACLES

[DK]

A Dorling Kindersley Book

Editors Miranda Smith
Stephen Setford

Senior art editor Chris Scollen

Art director Roger Priddy
Managing editor Ann Kramer

Editorial consultant Julian Holland
Production Shelagh Gibson

First published in Great Britain in 1992
by Dorling Kindersley Limited,
9 Henrietta Street, London WC2E 8PS

Copyright © 1992 Dorling Kindersley Limited,
London

All rights reserved. No part of this publication may be reproduced, stored in a retrieval system, or transmitted in any form or by any means, electronic, mechanical, photocopying, recording or otherwise, without the prior permission of the copyright owner.

A CIP catalogue record for this book is available from the British Library.

ISBN 0-86318-815-X

Colour Separations by DOT Gradations Limited
Printed in Spain by Artes Graficas; Toledo S.A.
D.L.TO:32-1992

56	MOVING GOODS
58	RIDING THE RAILS
60	AT TOP SPEED
62	DOWN THE LINE
64	INDEX

A TRANSPORT REVOLUTION

Every day, in countries across the globe, hundreds of thousands of people travel by train. Yet 200 years ago, such journeys were impossible. The trains that have opened up new worlds for us ran first in Britain at the beginning of the 19th century. European and North American engineers were quick to adopt the idea of putting steam-powered trains on tracks, and travel by train spread to most

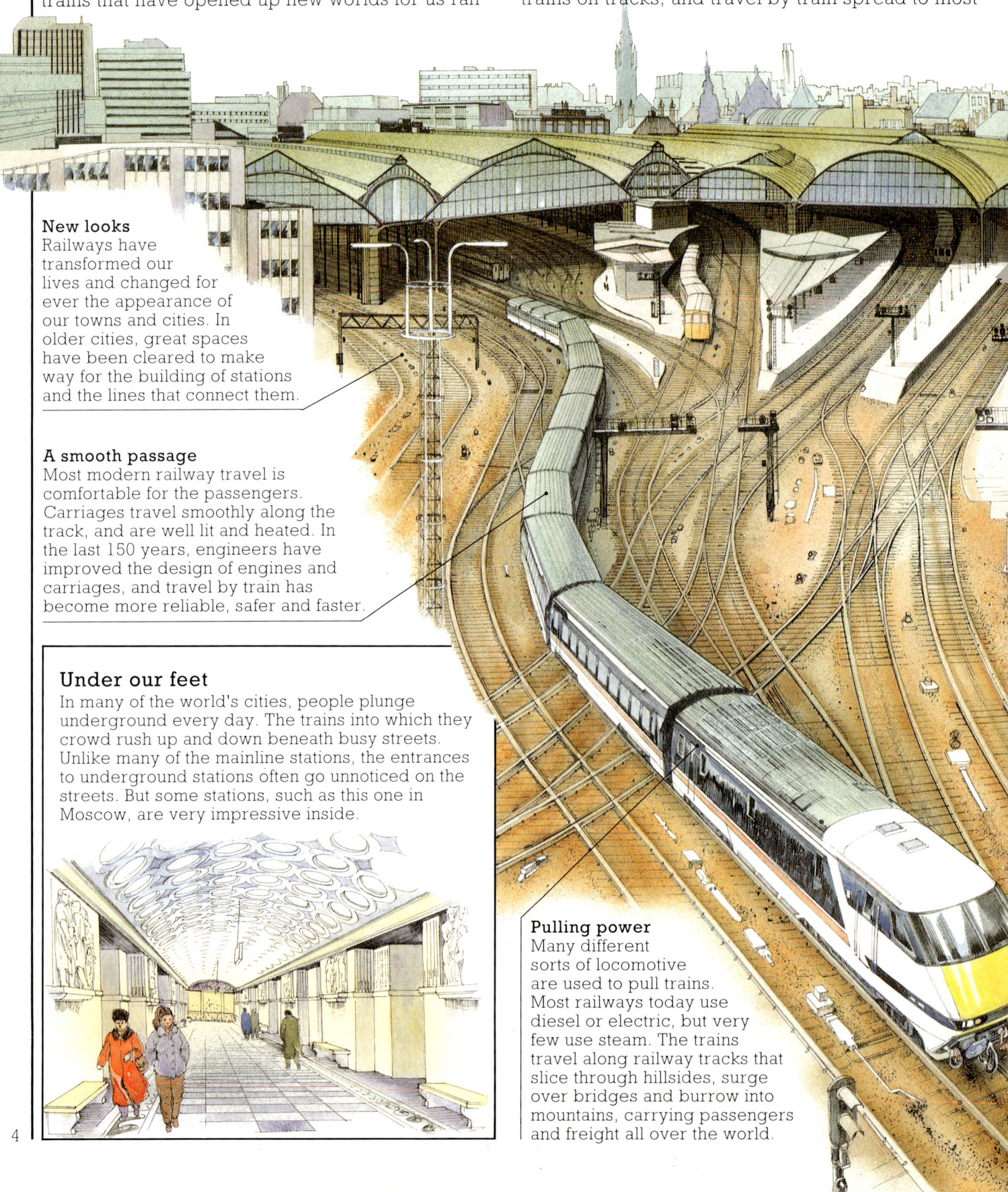

New looks
Railways have transformed our lives and changed for ever the appearance of our towns and cities. In older cities, great spaces have been cleared to make way for the building of stations and the lines that connect them.

A smooth passage
Most modern railway travel is comfortable for the passengers. Carriages travel smoothly along the track, and are well lit and heated. In the last 150 years, engineers have improved the design of engines and carriages, and travel by train has become more reliable, safer and faster.

Under our feet
In many of the world's cities, people plunge underground every day. The trains into which they crowd rush up and down beneath busy streets. Unlike many of the mainline stations, the entrances to underground stations often go unnoticed on the streets. But some stations, such as this one in Moscow, are very impressive inside.

Pulling power
Many different sorts of locomotive are used to pull trains. Most railways today use diesel or electric, but very few use steam. The trains travel along railway tracks that slice through hillsides, surge over bridges and burrow into mountains, carrying passengers and freight all over the world.

countries in the world. In the 20th century, diesel and electric powered engines have revolutionized railways, providing efficient high speed transport for both people and goods.

The start of a journey
Railways changed the world and the stations are the gateways to all that railways have to offer. These buildings were so important that sometimes whole new towns grew up around them.

The way in
Main line stations are all shapes and sizes. Many have been designed by famous architects and reflect the time in which they were built. Some are definitely meant to impress. For example, New York's Grand Central Station has a 46m (150ft) high domed ceiling!

Grand Central Station, New York

Melbourne Station, Australia

The Gare de Lyons, Paris

Bangkok Station, Thailand

Down the track
Today's railways are a vital link between people in different places. Because of railways it is possible to travel great distances, enjoy holidays in foreign places and buy goods made in distant countries.

THE FIRST TRAINS

A Greek inventor called Hero, who lived in Egypt nearly 2,000 years ago, first showed that steam could be used to make objects turn. To entertain people, he made a revolving metal ball that held water and was fixed over a fire. As the water boiled, it turned to steam which escaped through the jets. This spun the ball round.

It was not until the beginning of the 18th century that steam was used successfully to carry out heavy work. The coal and tin mines of the time were being dug deeper, and their products were increasingly in demand, but flooding in mines was a real problem. Steam power was used to work the pumps which kept the mine shafts free of water.

Engineers also realized that wagons carrying heavy materials such as coal were more easily pulled along rails than along the bumpy roads of the time. These early tramways were made of wood and the wagons that ran along them were pulled by horses.

The need for railways
By the end of the 18th century, great improvements in the iron and steel industries resulted in stronger and more reliable steam engines being made. Engineers like James Watt improved the engines and found ways to power many different types of machine.

The first steam vehicles
James Watt believed it was too dangerous to use steam power to move vehicles - he was afraid of explosion. But his foreman, William Murdoch, was one of the first to build steam carriages. In 1769, the Frenchman Nicholas Cugnot amazed crowds in Paris with a machine that managed 3kph (2mph) before falling over and blowing up. The authorities seized its remains and put Cugnot in prison.

A forceful man
Richard Trevithick was born in 1771, the son of a Cornish tin mine manager. He was very strong and could hurl a sledge-hammer over a mine engine house. He was a clever inventor as well as a forceful man. He worked on improving Watt's steam engines and, in 1801, built his first full-size locomotive. This machine ran on the road but ended by crashing into a house.

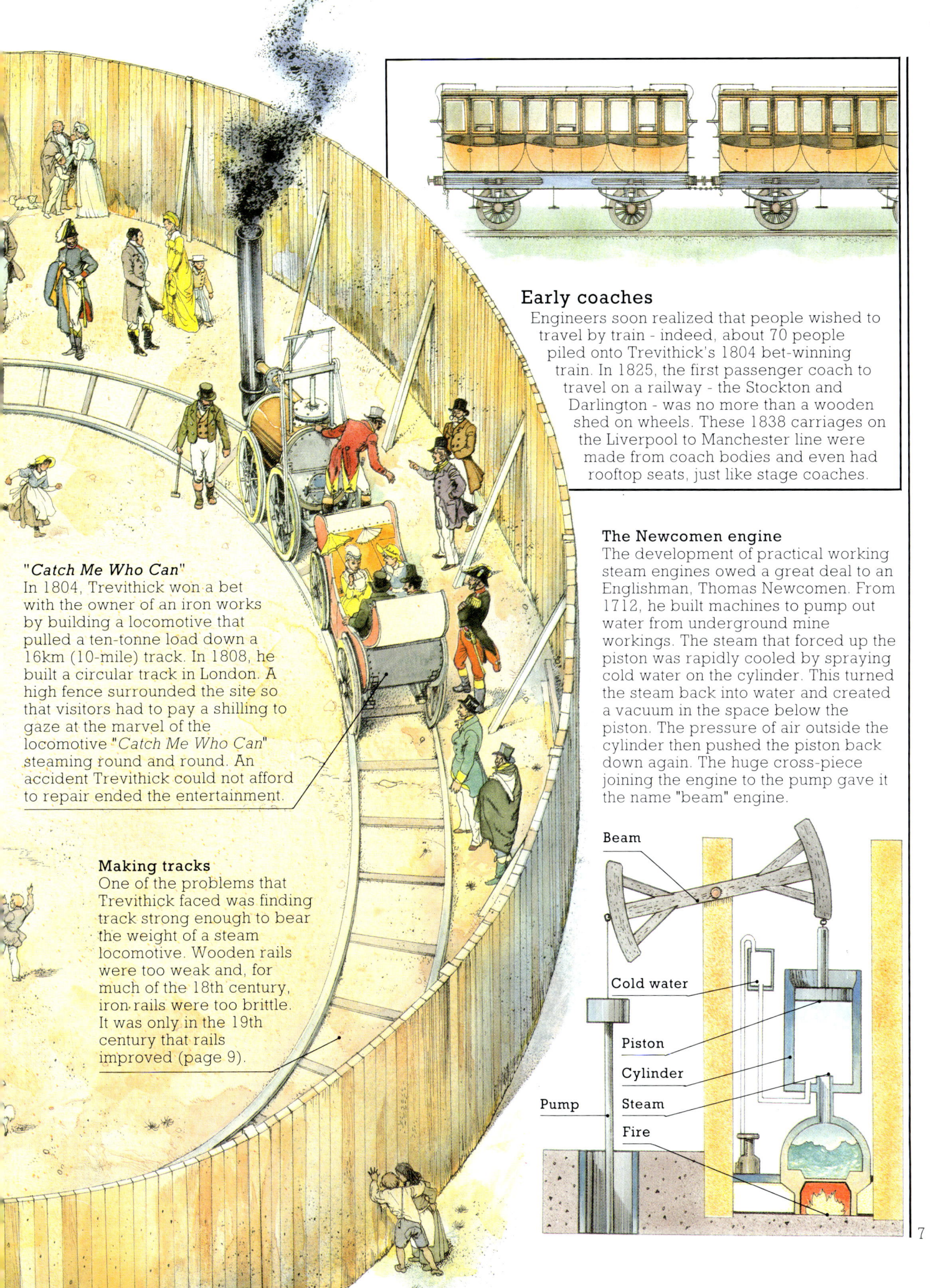

Early coaches
Engineers soon realized that people wished to travel by train - indeed, about 70 people piled onto Trevithick's 1804 bet-winning train. In 1825, the first passenger coach to travel on a railway - the Stockton and Darlington - was no more than a wooden shed on wheels. These 1838 carriages on the Liverpool to Manchester line were made from coach bodies and even had rooftop seats, just like stage coaches.

"Catch Me Who Can"
In 1804, Trevithick won a bet with the owner of an iron works by building a locomotive that pulled a ten-tonne load down a 16km (10-mile) track. In 1808, he built a circular track in London. A high fence surrounded the site so that visitors had to pay a shilling to gaze at the marvel of the locomotive "Catch Me Who Can" steaming round and round. An accident Trevithick could not afford to repair ended the entertainment.

The Newcomen engine
The development of practical working steam engines owed a great deal to an Englishman, Thomas Newcomen. From 1712, he built machines to pump out water from underground mine workings. The steam that forced up the piston was rapidly cooled by spraying cold water on the cylinder. This turned the steam back into water and created a vacuum in the space below the piston. The pressure of air outside the cylinder then pushed the piston back down again. The huge cross-piece joining the engine to the pump gave it the name "beam" engine.

Making tracks
One of the problems that Trevithick faced was finding track strong enough to bear the weight of a steam locomotive. Wooden rails were too weak and, for much of the 18th century, iron rails were too brittle. It was only in the 19th century that rails improved (page 9).

THE AGE OF STEAM

Despite the work of Richard Trevithick, steam power still seemed too unreliable, too dangerous and too costly. Also, heavy steam locomotives soon wrecked the wooden track commonly used at the time. Even when iron plates were fastened to the wood, the track was still not strong enough.

The first railway that regularly carried fare-paying passengers was the Welsh Swansea to Mumbles line of 1806, which used horses. The first North American railway line opened in 1795, with horses pulling trucks laden with material to build the State House in Boston. When wars between Napoleon's France and other European countries caused the price of horse feed to rise, steam power began to seem attractive. In 1812, the Middleton line at Leeds in England became the first railway to regularly use steam locomotives. By this time, too, English iron makers had learned how to produce stronger track. William Jessop designed iron rails in sections 75cm (2ft 6in) long with smooth tops along which shaped or "flanged" wheels ran.

Getting up steam
In England in 1825, the Stockton to Darlington line, the world's first public railway, opened. Horses pulled most of the traffic, but from time to time, a steam locomotive was used. The engineer who provided the locomotive was George Stephenson and he named his engine Locomotion. *The engine could pull wagons crowded with hundreds of people, as well as loads of coal, iron and corn, at 8kph (5mph). Soon, Stephenson and his fellow engineers designed more powerful engines.*

Business interests
In the 18th century, the north-east of England was an important coal-mining area. Mine owners were keen to sell more coal to expanding cities and industries, but moving the heavy coal was a real problem. Many of the early pioneers of steam power worked for collieries, and many mine owners gave them the money to develop their ideas. For example, Edward Pease, a Quaker businessman, helped George Stephenson and his son Robert set up a locomotive-building works.

George Stephenson
George Stephenson was born in 1781. His home was a railwayside cottage and his father was a colliery fireman. George was soon working for Nicholas Wood at Killingworth Colliery, where he began to build locomotives.

The *Rocket*
George Stephenson and his son Robert increased the engine power of the *Rocket* by leading the exhaust steam out through a narrow chimney. They also improved the heating power by passing through the iron boiler several tubes to carry the heat, instead of only one or two.

The first accident?
On 15 September 1830, the opening of the Liverpool to Manchester line was marred by a tragedy. Having climbed out of one train, William Huskisson, Liverpool's Member of Parliament, was hit and killed by the *Rocket* travelling up another track.

Puffing Billy
Puffing Billy took its name from the loud noise made by its exhaust steam. Built by William Hedley it served Wylam Colliery for around 50 years. Hedley proved that smooth driving wheels running on smooth track could pull heavy loads.

The Rainhill trials
In October 1829, an excited crowd gathered to watch four engines compete. The fastest, the *Novelty*, was built by John Braithwaite and John Ericcson, but it kept stopping. Timothy Burstall's *Perseverance* lacked power and Timothy Hackworth's *Sans Pareil* used great quantities of fuel and broke down. The *Rocket* steamed up and down the test track at around 22kph (14mph) and the Stephensons collected the £500 prize.

Novelty

Sans Pareil

Making tracks
At the beginning of the 19th century, iron rails usually rested on stone supports and if any of these sank, the track became uneven. In 1820, John Birkenshaw of Bedlington developed a process of making wrought iron rails that were longer than the earlier wooden rails. Stephenson adopted this improvement and, in cooperation with William Losh, designed rails that joined each other by means of overlapping end sections. The joints were stronger and secured in chairs pinned to the base, which was often made of stone.

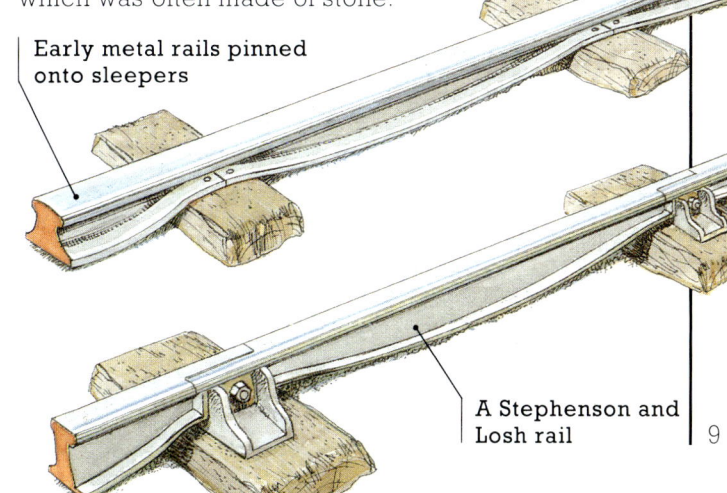

Early metal rails pinned onto sleepers

A Stephenson and Losh rail

MEN AT WORK

Railways dramatically altered the landscapes of the areas through which they passed. Inhabitants who saw railway surveyors at work knew that close behind them followed a great army of men ready to change the look of town and country to suit the railways. It needed several thousand men to build an important railway. The arrival of so many strangers often greatly alarmed the people living in the area nearby. The job of finding and organizing these workers, or "navvies", was not easy. Railway contractors like Thomas Brassey who were good at such work were able to make a lot of money. Brassey's men built lines not only in Britain but in other parts of Europe and in Australia and Argentina.

Altering the landscape
Railways need reasonably level ground to run over. Early lines had to follow the gentlest of slopes, as the locomotives of the time were not powerful enough to grip the track well on a hill. Navvies cut away hilly earth, drained wet land and built up the ground to make embankments. They also cleared away housing and put up viaducts to carry the lines into towns and cities.

Tools of the trade
The navvies worked with simple tools, cutting into the ground with picks, shovelling out the earth, and loading it into wheelbarrows. When faced with rock, they used gunpowder to blow it to pieces, then they trundled barrow-loads of earth and rock to horse-drawn wagons. The wagons often ran on rails to the workings, and took away earth and rock, dumping it where it was needed to make an embankment.

Barrow runs
When earth and stones were not needed, they were dumped. Horses pulled the barrows up with ropes which ran over pulleys. The men guided the barrows up the wooden planks of the barrow runs. This was difficult work that only the strongest navvies could do. A man who fell could be buried alive.

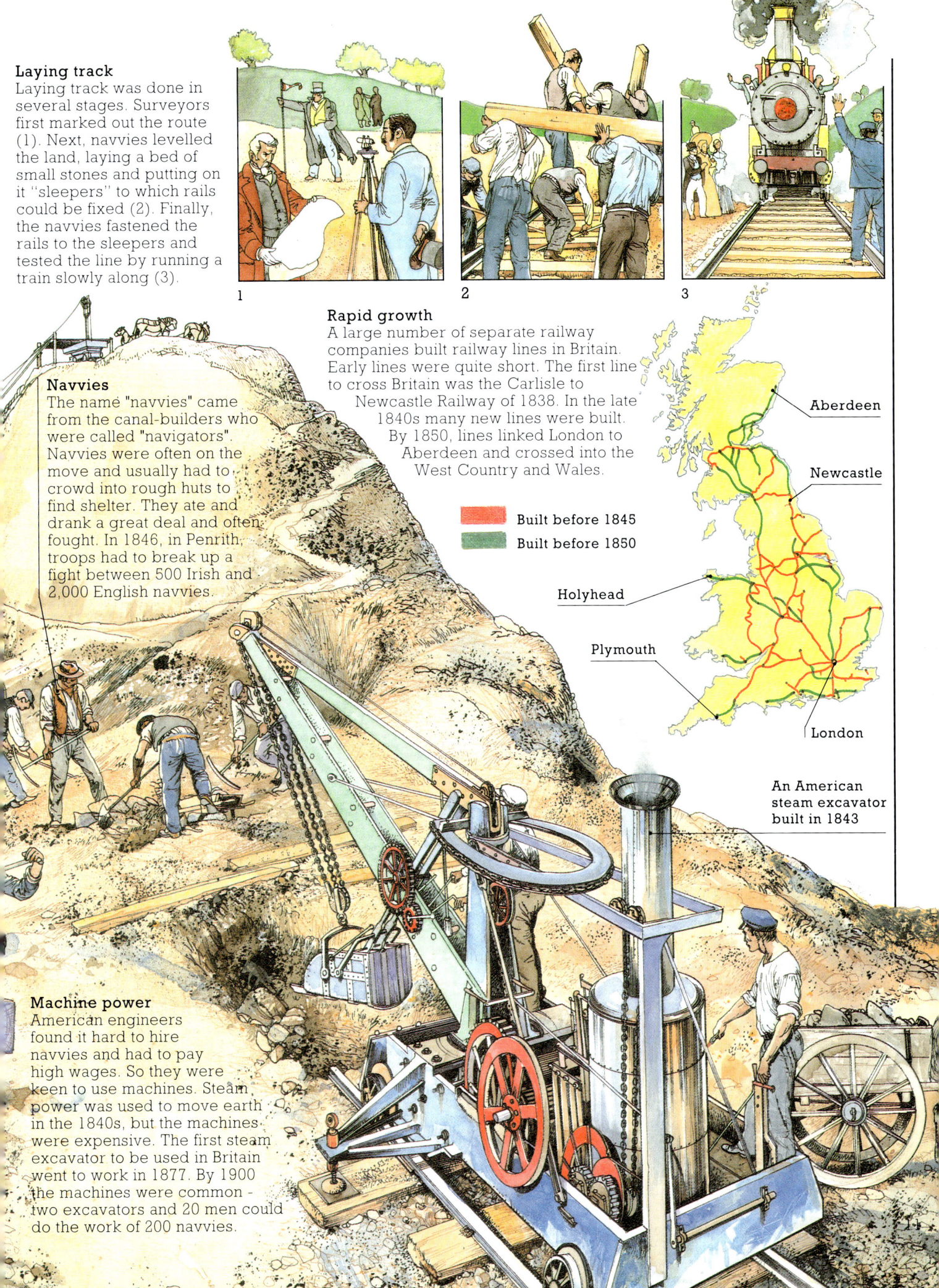

Laying track
Laying track was done in several stages. Surveyors first marked out the route (1). Next, navvies levelled the land, laying a bed of small stones and putting on it "sleepers" to which rails could be fixed (2). Finally, the navvies fastened the rails to the sleepers and tested the line by running a train slowly along (3).

Navvies
The name "navvies" came from the canal-builders who were called "navigators". Navvies were often on the move and usually had to crowd into rough huts to find shelter. They ate and drank a great deal and often fought. In 1846, in Penrith, troops had to break up a fight between 500 Irish and 2,000 English navvies.

Rapid growth
A large number of separate railway companies built railway lines in Britain. Early lines were quite short. The first line to cross Britain was the Carlisle to Newcastle Railway of 1838. In the late 1840s many new lines were built. By 1850, lines linked London to Aberdeen and crossed into the West Country and Wales.

■ Built before 1845
■ Built before 1850

An American steam excavator built in 1843

Machine power
American engineers found it hard to hire navvies and had to pay high wages. So they were keen to use machines. Steam power was used to move earth in the 1840s, but the machines were expensive. The first steam excavator to be used in Britain went to work in 1877. By 1900 the machines were common – two excavators and 20 men could do the work of 200 navvies.

A CHANGE OF GAUGE

The width of railway track, or gauge, is not the same in every part of the world. In Britain, North America, nearly all of Western Europe and China, the lines are 1,435mm (4ft 8½in) apart. In India, Pakistan and Argentina, the width is 1,676mm (5ft 6in), whilst in Russia it is 1,520mm (just under 5ft). There are also a number of lines that are very narrow (page 52).

This confusion of gauges dates back to the beginning of railways. George Stephenson adopted the "standard gauge" of 1,435mm, but not all British builders followed the same gauge. Isambard Kingdom Brunel, for example, developed a railway built to a 2,133mm (7ft) gauge.

Broad gauge track of 2,133mm (7ft) width

The battle of the gauges
Brunel's broad gauge Great Western Railway opened in 1838. Where this line linked up to standard gauge track, passengers had to change trains. In 1845, a parliamentary commission investigated the problem and the GWR finally converted to standard gauge in 1892.

Brunel argued in vain that his wider lines provided greater speed and safety

The broad gauge
Many of the locomotives on Brunel's Great Western Railway were built by Daniel Gooch and were able to rush along the broad level track at high speeds. The wide coaches could seat nine people along one side, whereas standard gauge coaches only had space for five.

Enemies of the railway
Not everybody welcomed the coming of railways. Canal transport suffered because railway travel was so much quicker. Stagecoach and wagon services were very badly hit. Three months after it opened, the Liverpool to Manchester line had put half the local stage coaches out of business! Many landowners and farmers hated the noise, smoke and dirt and feared locomotives would frighten their animals. Members of the House of Lords grumbled that steam engines would ruin their hunting and shooting. Even Queen Victoria - a regular railway traveller - would not let a railway travel on her land at Balmoral, Scotland.

Signals
When speeds increased, warning signals became essential. Railway managers often used officers from the army and navy to run their railways, so they set up a network of railway policemen who, as well as helping to keep the peace, signalled to the train drivers. Some used flags, others just their hands and arms.

"Caution" "Defect on the rails" "All clear"

Sometimes, there was terrible confusion when the passengers changed trains

The standard gauge
The 1,435mm (4ft 8½ in) track came about almost by accident. It was the gauge used on many wagonways in the north-east of Britain, so locomotive builders in the area, including the Stephensons, used it when building engines for local mines.

Standard gauge track

Feeling was so strong against some railway lines, that people stood in the path of some trains

THE PEOPLE TRAVEL

During the second half of the 19th century, the building of railway lines altered living and working conditions, and brought new opportunities for holidays. Railways changed the foods people ate, the clothes they wore, even the time at which they set their clocks and watches! Trains could carry large numbers of people and great quantities of goods over long distances. Those who could afford to travel by train could now live further away from their work, and "suburbs" of pleasant houses with gardens grew up near cities. Even if they could not travel, people could still find out more about the rest of the world, for railways carried national newspapers, as well as letters and parcels.

Holidays by the sea
The wealthy often went on holiday for many weeks, while working people enjoyed day trips or short breaks. The seaside was one of the most popular areas for holidays. Quiet little fishing villages grew in size and many hotels and guest-houses were built. A number of places added other attractions - piers, funfairs, theatres.

A Victorian scene
An English railway station around 1900 was a bustling place. Porters wheeled trolleys or carried passengers' cases and hat-boxes. It was noisy and dirty, for steam trains hissed out clouds of smoke that stained the glass roofs and scattered specks of black soot onto clothing.

Timetable

In charge
The station was run by the station master. He checked the station clock for the correct "railway time". Before railways, different places in the same country had their own local time. But these gradually vanished as railway "standard" time took over.

Growth and expansion
Railway stations rapidly developed into important centres of local life. Railway companies began to construct large buildings, improving their appearance with beautifully decorated ironwork. Book and newspaper sellers set up stalls in the stations while new businesses opened up nearby.

Cook's tours
In 1840, Thomas Cook began organizing holidays by train all over Europe. Other people soon copied the idea. Organized sports were also popular, and people travelled to places where they could play, and events like race meetings, or football matches.

A better diet
Before railways, it had not been possible to move large amounts of food because travel was so slow and costly, and fresh food rotted. Trains meant that fruit, fish, vegetables, meat, milk and eggs could be transported easily and people's diets improved.

Porters carried passengers' luggage as well as helping them find the correct carriage

HEADING WEST

Eight million people lived in the United States in the early 19th century. In the following years, many more arrived from Europe. In the 1840s, for example, over four million people poured into the country. The first railways were built in the eastern United States, where most people had settled. As the population of the country increased, so more and more people moved west, searching for good land to farm and pushing aside the native Americans who already lived there. The railways spread slowly westwards too. The US government was keen to support the businessmen who wanted to build railway lines, because railways helped to unite a vast land.

Despite the odds
Railway builders faced all sorts of obstacles. Great mountain ranges stood in the way; deserts had to be crossed and forests cleared. In 1856, the Rock Island Line Company tackled the vast Mississippi River. They built a huge 483m (1,583ft) bridge across it. The way west was now open.

Setting up home
When the men who built the lines across North America moved into new areas, there were no towns or cities for them to visit, so they had to carry all they needed with them. Along the finished line, little towns grew up, with stagecoaches to carry passengers to places not on the railroad line. Shops opened up and so did saloons providing drink and entertainment.

Travelling towns
The trains themselves transported all the materials needed to build a new line. They also carried food, clothes and tools. The Union Pacific's construction crews sometimes slept in specially built "bunkhouse cars". The Union Pacific trains were often pulled by sturdy little *Pony* locomotives. These engines burned wood, as there was usually a good supply of timber nearby, and coal was harder to obtain.

Bunkhouse car

Promontory Point
Sacramento
Omaha
Central Pacific
Union Pacific

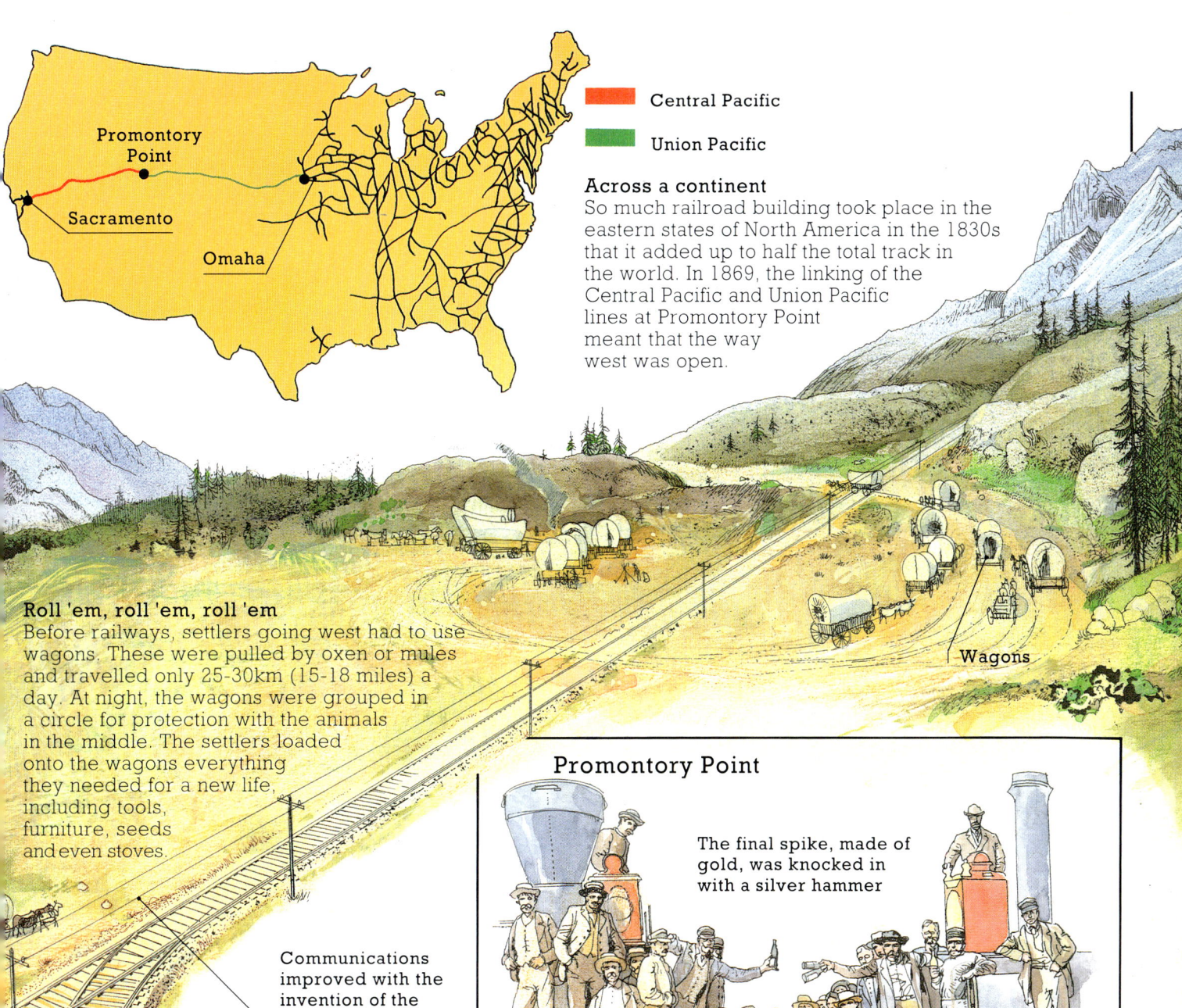

Across a continent

So much railroad building took place in the eastern states of North America in the 1830s that it added up to half the total track in the world. In 1869, the linking of the Central Pacific and Union Pacific lines at Promontory Point meant that the way west was open.

Wagons
Communications improved with the invention of the telegraph system

Roll 'em, roll 'em, roll 'em

Before railways, settlers going west had to use wagons. These were pulled by oxen or mules and travelled only 25-30km (15-18 miles) a day. At night, the wagons were grouped in a circle for protection with the animals in the middle. The settlers loaded onto the wagons everything they needed for a new life, including tools, furniture, seeds and even stoves.

Building a network

Once the main line across the continent was finished, other lines were built. In 1880, the Kansas Pacific Line was linked to the main cross country route. Railroads meant that inland America was opened up. Chicago, for example, was a place where eleven railroads met. Hotel-keepers there provided roof-top telescopes so that their clients could look out for the arrival of important trains.

Promontory Point

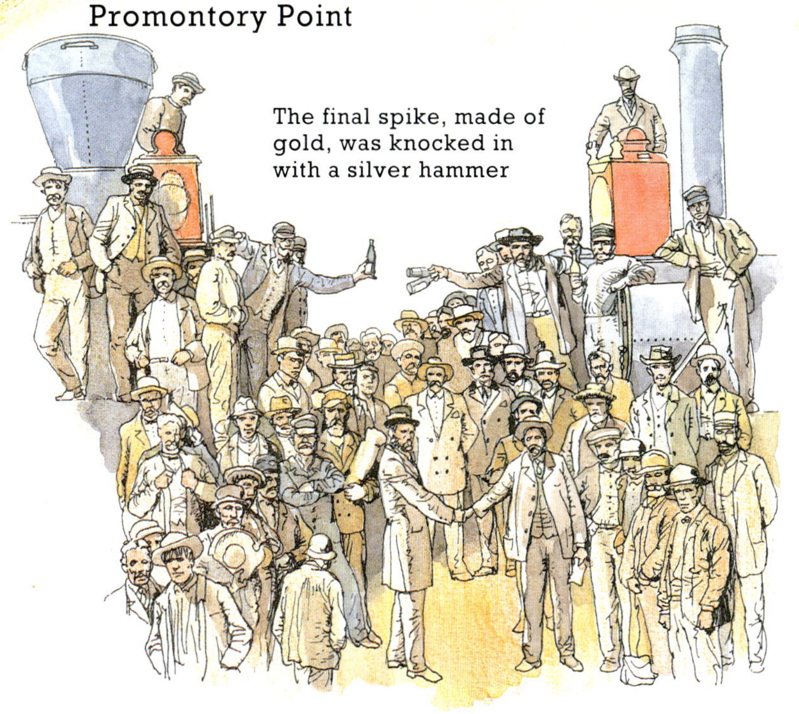

The final spike, made of gold, was knocked in with a silver hammer

On 10 May 1869, a special event was organized to celebrate the linking of the Central Pacific and Union Pacific lines at Promontory Point. The Central Pacific brought a train pulled by the *Jupiter*, while the Union Pacific used *Locomotive 119*. The Union Pacific had begun work in Omaha, Nebraska, in December 1863, using a team of workers that included 15 native American squaws. Work on the Central Pacific Railroad Company had begun in January 1863 at Sacramento, California. Labourers were in short supply there and the line's engineers brought in thousands of Chinese labourers to do the work.

UNDER ATTACK

The railways brought many benefits, but they also brought violence. The lines that spread west in the United States pushed into native American country and the peoples who lived there soon came to hate the "iron horse" - the name they gave to the train. It frightened the wild animals and led to the killing of the great herds of buffalo the native Americans needed for food and clothing. In 1876, Sitting Bull's Sioux defeated an army led by General Custer that was protecting work on the Northern Pacific line. This Battle of Little Bighorn was a rare native American success. However, nothing could stop the relentless drive of the railroads.

Robbery on the plains
Wealthy people travelled by train, and many of the railroads carried gold or other valuables. The result was that railways attracted robbers and gamblers. Some waited in railway towns to take money from travellers. Others went on board the trains and robbed fellow passengers. Some even attacked the trains while they were on the move.

Easy target
In 1870, six men boarded one of the Central Pacific trains in California. When the engine stopped for fuel and water the men held up the train, uncoupling the engine and the express car in which valuables were kept. They steamed further down the track before stopping and robbing the express car.

Fighting back
The native Americans tried to protect their lands and the buffalo (see above) by pulling up railway track. Sometimes they ambushed railroad men. Workers employed by the Kansas Pacific Line learned to carry and use guns, and the company even armed their passengers as well. In 1867, Cheyenne braves ambushed a telegraph repair crew, at Plum Creek, Nebraska, and killed all but one of them. William Thompson escaped by pretending to be dead, even when he was being scalped!

Cut off
The telegraph wires that ran beside the track linked up stations along the way. Some trains carried telegraphers with "box relays". These men could attach the box to the wires and send messages. Outlaws attacking trains often cut the wires to stop help being summoned.

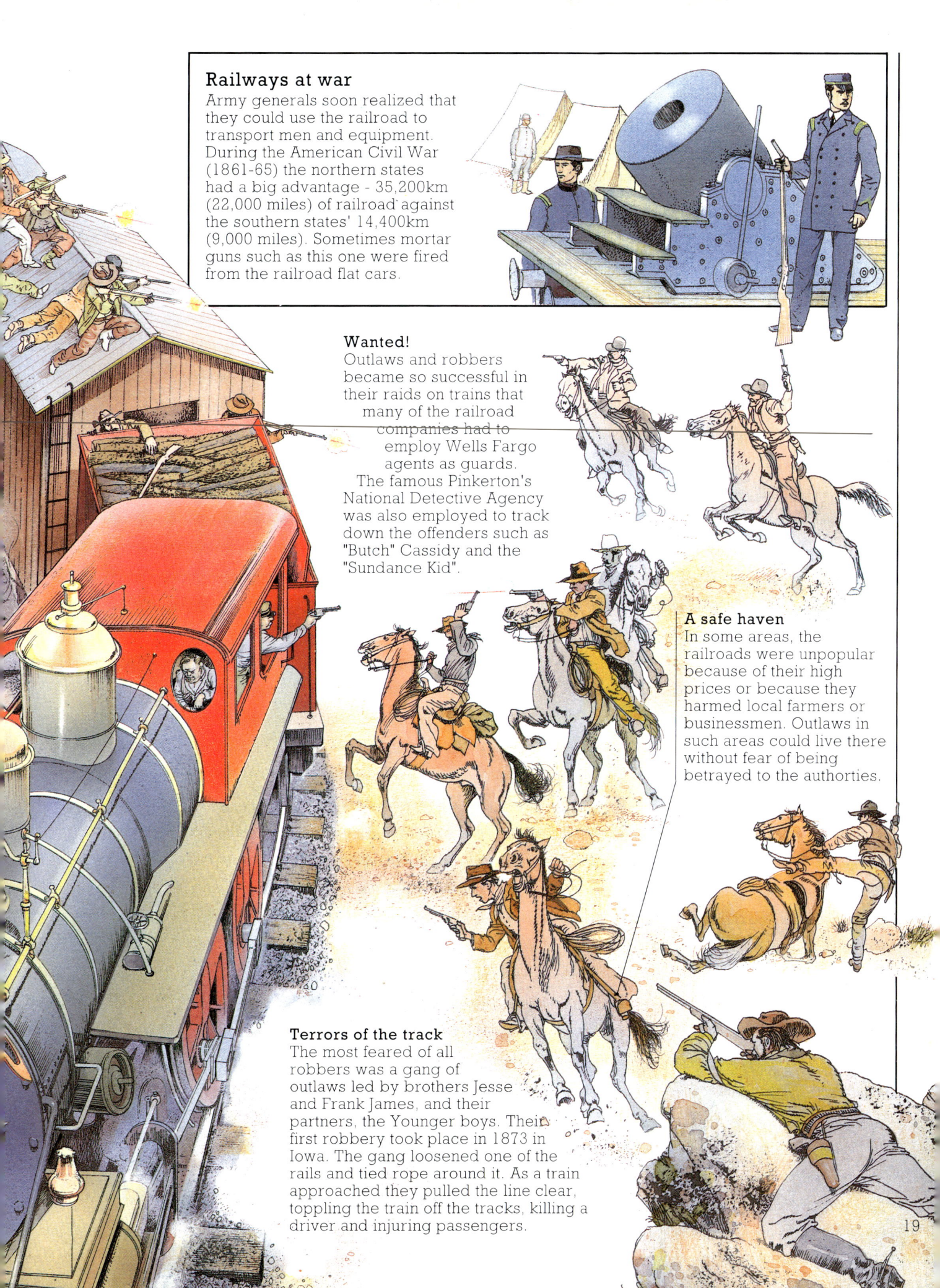

Railways at war
Army generals soon realized that they could use the railroad to transport men and equipment. During the American Civil War (1861-65) the northern states had a big advantage - 35,200km (22,000 miles) of railroad against the southern states' 14,400km (9,000 miles). Sometimes mortar guns such as this one were fired from the railroad flat cars.

Wanted!
Outlaws and robbers became so successful in their raids on trains that many of the railroad companies had to employ Wells Fargo agents as guards. The famous Pinkerton's National Detective Agency was also employed to track down the offenders such as "Butch" Cassidy and the "Sundance Kid".

A safe haven
In some areas, the railroads were unpopular because of their high prices or because they harmed local farmers or businessmen. Outlaws in such areas could live there without fear of being betrayed to the authorties.

Terrors of the track
The most feared of all robbers was a gang of outlaws led by brothers Jesse and Frank James, and their partners, the Younger boys. Their first robbery took place in 1873 in Iowa. The gang loosened one of the rails and tied rope around it. As a train approached they pulled the line clear, toppling the train off the tracks, killing a driver and injuring passengers.

COAST TO COAST

Inventors tried many different ways to make steam engines faster and more powerful, but the reasons the engines worked remained the same: heated water turns to steam and steam is a powerful force that can move heavy objects. This engine is the famous *Jupiter* that the Central Pacific Railroad used at Promontory Point. It had four driving wheels and four "bogey" wheels to guide the engine and keep it firmly on the track. Like many American engines, the *Jupiter* was fitted with a cowcatcher. This was an attachment that pushed cattle to one side of the track if they wandered into the path of a train. Cowcatchers were essential when trains crossed the grasslands of North America.

The *Jupiter* burned wood. This did not produce as much fierce heat as coal fire, but in North America it was plentiful and cheaper than coal. Wood-burning engines often gave out a shower of sparks with the smoke and steam. The sparks could set fire to forests and dry grasslands, so "spark arresters" were fitted to the chimneys to try and stop this happening.

Spark arrester

Lamp

Blast pipe

Cowcatcher

Steam pipe

A safety valve is built into the boiler to automatically release excess steam

The pistons
The steam is fed down the steam pipe to two cylinders at the front of the engine. The steam is released in bursts, first at one end of the cylinders, then at the other. The force of the steam pushes the pistons backwards and forwards. The pistons are joined to piston rods and then to connecting rods. These link onto the driving wheels, making them turn.

The boiler
The boiler is a strong metal tank filled with water. Fire tubes running through the boiler heat the water to make steam. It takes quite a while to get a steam locomotive going, as the flames in the firebox need time to build up heat in the fire tubes. More water is added from time to time as the water in the boiler is used up by being turned to steam.

The dome
Steam from the boiler collects in the dome. The engineer driving the train decides when the steam pressure is strong enough to move the pistons and turn the wheels. He opens a valve that lets steam flow out of the dome along the steam pipe to the cylinders. Steam that has done its job of moving the pistons is released through the blast pipe.

Trekking west
Regular services across the United States began soon after the Central Pacific and Union Pacific lines were joined. The US government gave the railroad companies grants of land, so the companies advertized in Europe, trying to persuade people to come to America. They wanted to profit from carrying these people west and selling them the land. Trains like the Jupiter *carried thousands of European immigrants to settle in the mid- and far west.*

The tender
A steam locomotive needs fuel. This is kept in a "tender", a wagon next to the engine. The fireman keeps the flames in the firebox burning by shovelling or lifting fuel onto the fire. Wood-burning locomotives such as the *Jupiter* needed large tenders in which to carry their bulky fuel and had to stop regularly to take on more.

A dangerous living
Railroad cattle towns were wild places. The railroad companies employed men to protect their cargoes in the station as well as on the journey. Abilene, for example, was a very dangerous place to live in until James Butler Hickok became Marshal. He had already killed 43 people and earned the nickname of "Wild Bill". By the time his work in Abilene was over he had shot 57 more.

The cattle towns
The railroads helped the growth of the cattle trade. Cattle-transporting railroad stops such as Abilene, Ellsworth and Hays City solved the problem of how to take cattle through farmlands where settlers had put up fences.

Passenger comfort
Wealthy people able to pay 1,000 dollars could travel across North America in express trains that took four or five days to get from Omaha to western California. Those who could not afford the first class fares travelled in slower trains that took six or seven days. Finally, there were immigrant trains that carried newcomers to North America. The immigrants paid $40 for the trip and travelled on wooden board seats packed in 90 to a car.

Most people travelled on mixed trains that included goods wagons as well as carriages and the engine

A change of clothes
People coming to settle in the United States brought all their possessions with them. But wealthy Americans travelling on the trans-continental line carried plenty of luggage too. Guide books suggested that ladies carry spring clothes for the first part of the journey west, winter clothes for use as the trains steamed over the mountains, and summer clothes for California.

Taking a break
The trains crossing America stopped at around 200 stations and water tanks. At some of these the passengers were allowed only 30 minutes to order and eat food. They had to listen for the conductor's whistle and cry of "All aboard".

Basic comforts
Passengers with enough money were soon able to travel in comfortable carriages designed by George Pullman. However, the carriages in which settlers travelled were very basic and often had a stove at one end. Native Americans rode in the baggage cars, or on the steps at the ends of the carriages.

Entertainment
The first railroad travellers across the continent watched wild animals and sometimes fired their guns at them. Travellers played games to pass the time. Some Pullmans had organs in them and musicians gave concerts for the passengers. On Sunday, there was usually a religious service held in one of the cars.

The travellers
In newly-settled western towns some passengers did not bother to buy tickets first. Travellers would board a train and then argue with the conductor about how much they should pay.

THE CIRCUS IS COMING

The railways brought a wide range of entertainment to the people. In 1796, Philip Astley put on a special show with horses and the circus was born! Others copied Astley and soon circuses and wild animal menageries went on tour. This meant walking long distances, and in much of Europe this remained the way of moving about until steam traction engines and, later, motor lorries were used. But the distances covered in North America were so huge that entertainers soon began to use the railroads.

In the middle of the 19th century, the great showmen Phineas Taylor Barnum and George F. Bailey developed great travelling shows that toured North America by rail and visited Europe. They moved their "big top" round America in 100-car trains.

A grand parade
Railways meant that travelling shows could cover huge distances. New towns in the mid- and far west were especially starved of entertainment and warmly welcomed such an event. The arrival of a circus was marked by the holding of a big parade. This advertized the circus and was good for business.

Animal magic
People enjoyed going to see wild animals. The first tiger was brought to the United States in 1789 and the first elephant arrived in 1796. Astley's circus used trained horses and dancing bears; performing dogs and camels were also popular.

Promotion
Before a circus train arrived, posters were put up in town promising a huge variety of amazing acts - in the case of Barnum and Bailey, "A veritable Tornado of Wonders".

Up main street
Some parades were more spectacular than others. In the 1860s, George Sanger's circus was touring Europe with parades of 100 horses, 42 wagons of wild animals, and a huge chariot pulled by 30 horses carrying his wife dressed as Britannia.

Circus acts
There were all kinds of entertainers in the circuses. They included tight-rope walkers, flying trapeze artists, and clowns. The American hunter Buffalo Bill Cody recruited hundreds of native Americans to perform in his Wild West show.

Catching the eye
The circus people tried to make their shows as spectacular as possible. The carriages in which the animals travelled were highly decorated and painted. Some of them had to be very strong to carry the large and powerful animals.

An easy load
The American G.R. Spalding invented special runways to load circus wagons onto railroad flatcars. W.C. Coup, who worked with Barnum and Bailey, perfected this loading and unloading technique.

HEAVY WORK

Many industries grew up in the 19th century, as more coal and iron were mined. Heavy goods had been very difficult to move by land so large industries needed to be by the sea, by canal, or by rivers so that boats could be used to transport goods. But railways could reach inland to wherever they were needed, to coalfields and places where iron ore was mined. The new railways played a major part in the Industrial Revolution, carrying heavy goods, speeding up transportation and creating a demand for steel and iron to make new railroads. New towns grew up, like Birmingham, Alabama, in the USA. By the late 19th century, Germany too, with its huge reserves of coal, was becoming a leading industrial nation, with railways linking its industries, farmland, towns and cities.

Industrial growth
Germany's railways linked her iron and steel industries to her coalfields. The railways' own need of coal and iron helped develop those industries. Some improvements to railways benefited other industries: Krupps of Essen used the stronger steel developed for rails and wheels to make cannons.

Materials in
Developing industries needed huge quantities of supplies. Train loads of building materials, of raw wool, jute and cotton for textile factories, and of iron ore too, rolled endlessly into growing towns. So did the food and other supplies needed by the industrial workers.

Nasmyth's steam hammer
Iron is made stronger by being repeatedly hammered. In 1839, James Nasmyth invented a steam hammer to help Isambard Brunel (page 27) make a huge iron shaft for the paddle wheels of his ship, *Great Britain*. The steam hammer was soon being used to make iron bars for tracks in far larger quantities than the "tilt" hammers ever managed.

Products out
Many of the things made in early factories were for the railways themselves. Locomotives, wagons and carriages were needed, so works like Borsig of Berlin developed. Thousands of kilometres of track were needed as well as the metal parts that were bolted together to make bridges.

A changing landscape

The new industries developed by the railways altered the appearance of the landscape. Tall factory chimneys and the chimneys of thousands of workers' homes poured out smoke from fires supplied by trainloads of coal. Older cities changed shape as housing was smashed down to let in the railway lines. The building of three railways into London made 150,000 people homeless!

Railways and steamships

The steamship the *Great Eastern* first set sail in 1858. The great railway bridge builder Isambard Kingdom Brunel designed this vessel, but died eight days after the launch. The idea of using steam to move ships developed at much the same time as the steam locomotive. Paddle wheels were used at first, and continued to be useful on rivers and lakes. But in rough seas they tipped out of the water, so propellers proved more reliable. Railways helped make steamships successful by bringing people and goods to the ports.

Workers

Railways employed huge numbers of people, including thousands who lived in railway towns where engines were made and mended. Workers' lives began to be ruled by machines. Yet by bringing a wide variety of cheaper food and cheap clothing, railways improved people's standard of living.

STRANGE TRAINS

Extraordinary engines had to be designed to solve unusual problems. Where railway lines climbed up and down steep slopes and crossed deep gorges, engineers often had to think up unusual designs for their engines (pages 52-53). The search for speed led to the building of locomotives with enormous driving wheels, because a piston can turn a big wheel as quickly as a small wheel, but a big wheel travels further. On the American Baltimore and Ohio Railroad, engines were run that looked rather like camels! They had a "hump" - the driver's cab - placed right on top of a long and narrow boiler.

The engineers who struggled to design the first locomotives sometimes came up with very odd inventions. The Englishman William Brunton amazed people in 1815 with a steam locomotive pushed along the rails by two huge legs, complete with ankle joints and feet. Unfortunately, on one disastrous day it blew up, killing its crew and several people who were peering closely at it.

An odd assortment
These two pages show some of the more unusual engines and railway tracks of the 19th century. Although peculiar, they were all invented to solve particular sets of problems. All ran successfully for a number of years and some were even copied.

Trains with teeth
When track has to be built up and down very steep slopes, ordinary wheels slip and slide too easily. Early engineers designed an extra rail in a rack shape - a cog wheel with teeth fitted into projections on the rack. Rack railway systems were especially popular in Switzerland.

The "Daddy Long Legs"
Imagine a train that has to be fitted with lifeboats and lifebelts! In 1896, just such a train ran at Brighton, in England. The track along which it ran was 5,486mm (18ft) wide and 4.4km (nearly 3 miles) long, and it carried its passengers through 4.5m (15ft) of sea water. It was built by Magnus Volk and ran for five years before the damage done by rough water battering the rails led to the line being abandoned.

This steam-powered "rack and pinion" train is one of two that operate today in Austria

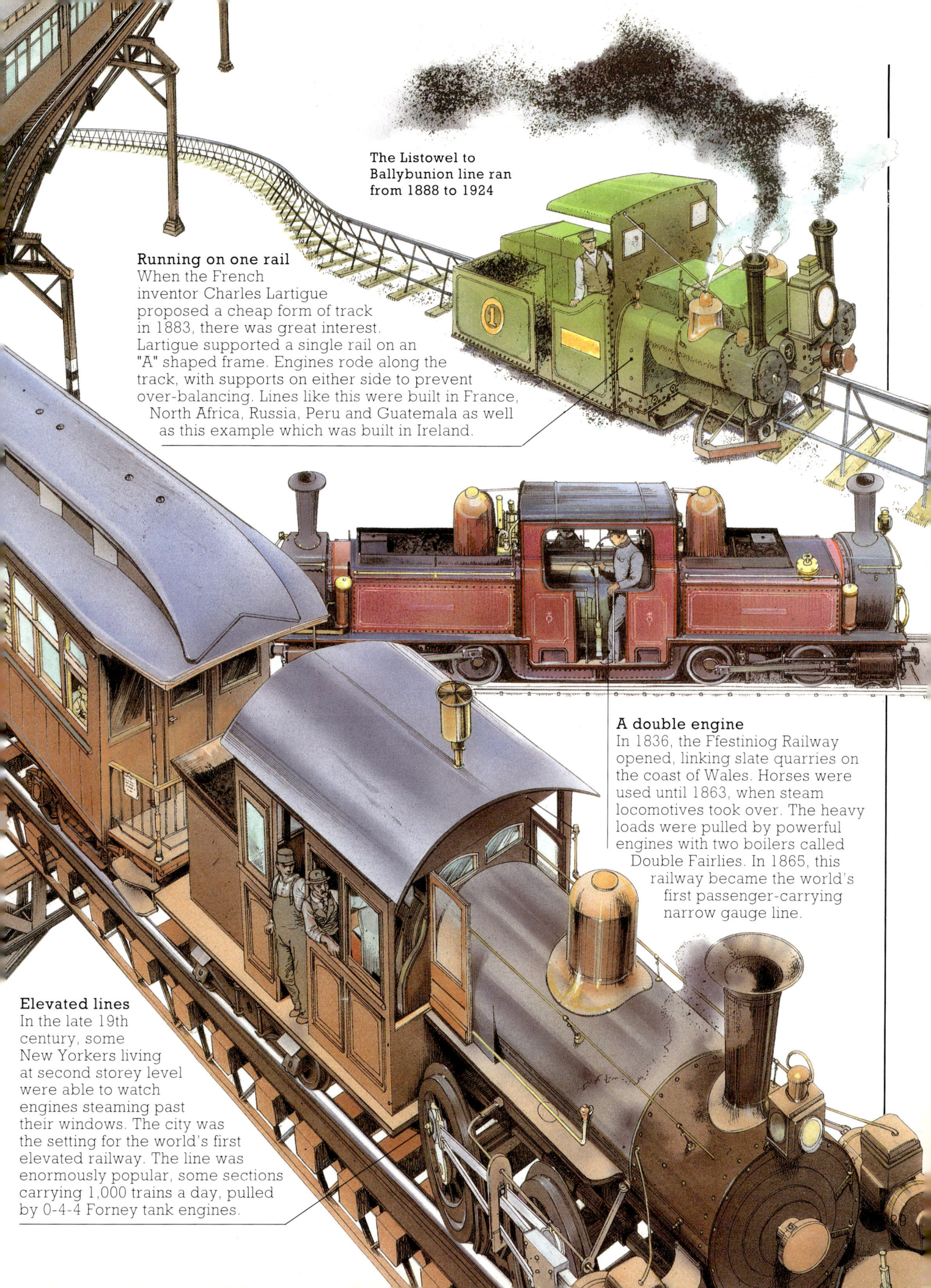

The Listowel to Ballybunion line ran from 1888 to 1924

Running on one rail
When the French inventor Charles Lartigue proposed a cheap form of track in 1883, there was great interest. Lartigue supported a single rail on an "A" shaped frame. Engines rode along the track, with supports on either side to prevent over-balancing. Lines like this were built in France, North Africa, Russia, Peru and Guatemala as well as this example which was built in Ireland.

A double engine
In 1836, the Ffestiniog Railway opened, linking slate quarries on the coast of Wales. Horses were used until 1863, when steam locomotives took over. The heavy loads were pulled by powerful engines with two boilers called Double Fairlies. In 1865, this railway became the world's first passenger-carrying narrow gauge line.

Elevated lines
In the late 19th century, some New Yorkers living at second storey level were able to watch engines steaming past their windows. The city was the setting for the world's first elevated railway. The line was enormously popular, some sections carrying 1,000 trains a day, pulled by 0-4-4 Forney tank engines.

THE AGE OF ROMANCE

On 4 October 1883, a Belgian businessman was walking anxiously up and down the platform of a Paris railway station. His name was Georges Nagelmackers and he had just risked all his money paying for the building of a brand new train. He planned to run a train right across Europe using the tracks of several countries. Many people told him this was impossible because it meant persuading quarrelling countries to agree to the plan. Moreover, Nagelmackers' train was as expensive a train as it was possible to build.

The Compagnie Internationale des Wagons Lits, Nagelmackers' company, was set up in 1876. By 1883, Nagelmackers had permission to take his train across eastern Europe to the Black Sea coast. The new train was called the *Orient Express*, a title that attracted great interest among wealthy travellers looking for adventure. So many secret agents used the train that it earned the nickname of the "Spies Express". The spies included the dancer Mata Hari, a German spy; and two agents who were killed by being pushed out of the carriages.

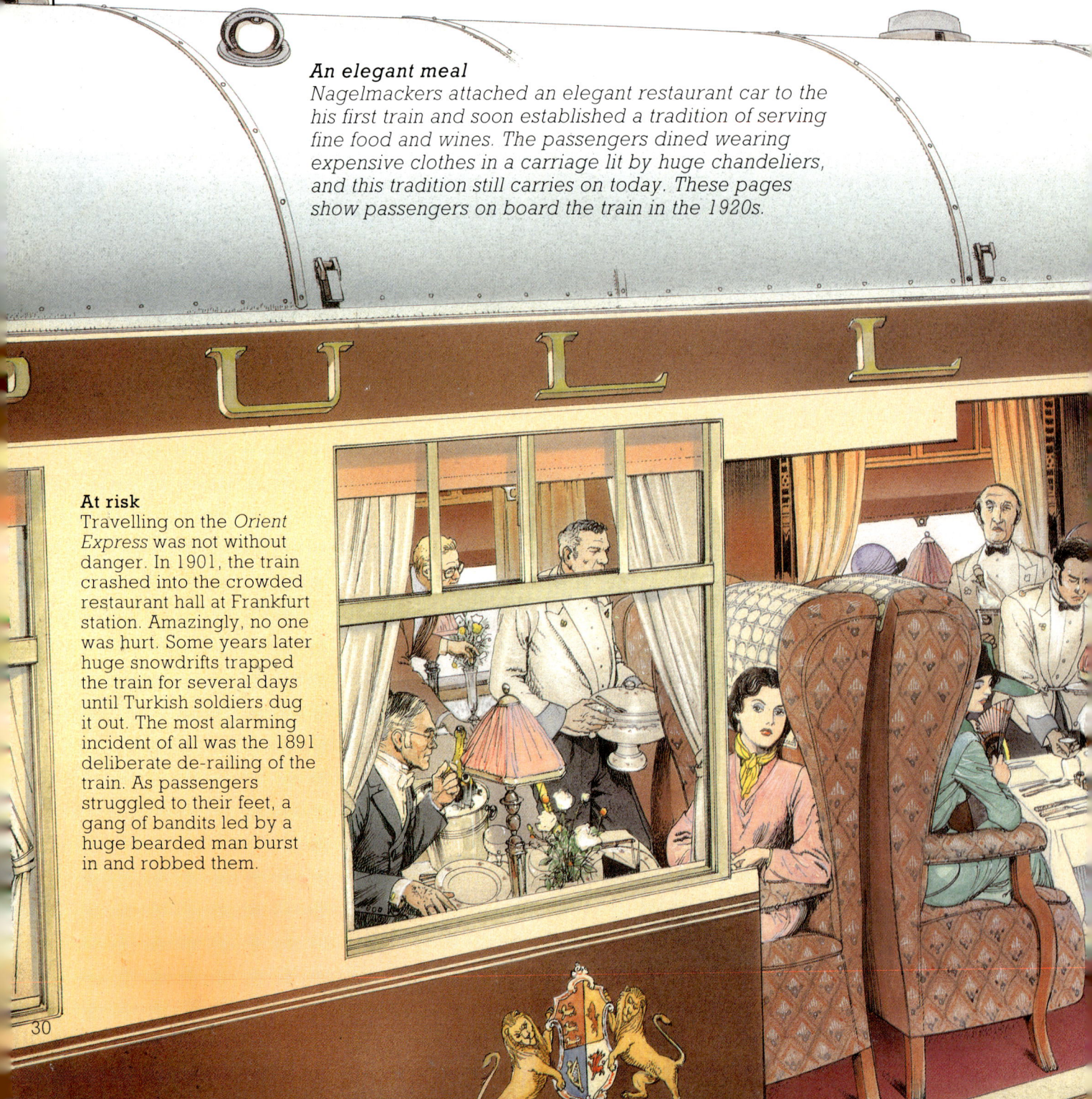

An elegant meal
Nagelmackers attached an elegant restaurant car to the his first train and soon established a tradition of serving fine food and wines. The passengers dined wearing expensive clothes in a carriage lit by huge chandeliers, and this tradition still carries on today. These pages show passengers on board the train in the 1920s.

At risk
Travelling on the *Orient Express* was not without danger. In 1901, the train crashed into the crowded restaurant hall at Frankfurt station. Amazingly, no one was hurt. Some years later huge snowdrifts trapped the train for several days until Turkish soldiers dug it out. The most alarming incident of all was the 1891 deliberate de-railing of the train. As passengers struggled to their feet, a gang of bandits led by a huge bearded man burst in and robbed them.

Engine   Tender   Baggage car

Food and drink
The first restaurant meal on the *Orient Express* was prepared on a gas stove in a tiny kitchen by a chef, three under chefs, three handymen and two cleaners. Today, the kitchen has the benefit of new technology, but it is still just as small.

Dressing up
The waiters serving meals on the first trip made by the *Orient Express* wore powdered wigs, tailcoats, breeches and silk stockings. However, passengers soon complained that the powder from the wigs fell on their food!

Decor
No expense was spared in fitting out the *Orient Express*. Panelling of the finest woods was carved into fanciful shapes. In the compartments, the armchairs were covered in soft Spanish leather while some of the walls were covered in silk.

The train
Nagelmackers provided the coaches, but the locomotives pulling them were owned by the different railway companies along whose track the train ran. The engines needed to be powerful, as the train had to move at high speed.

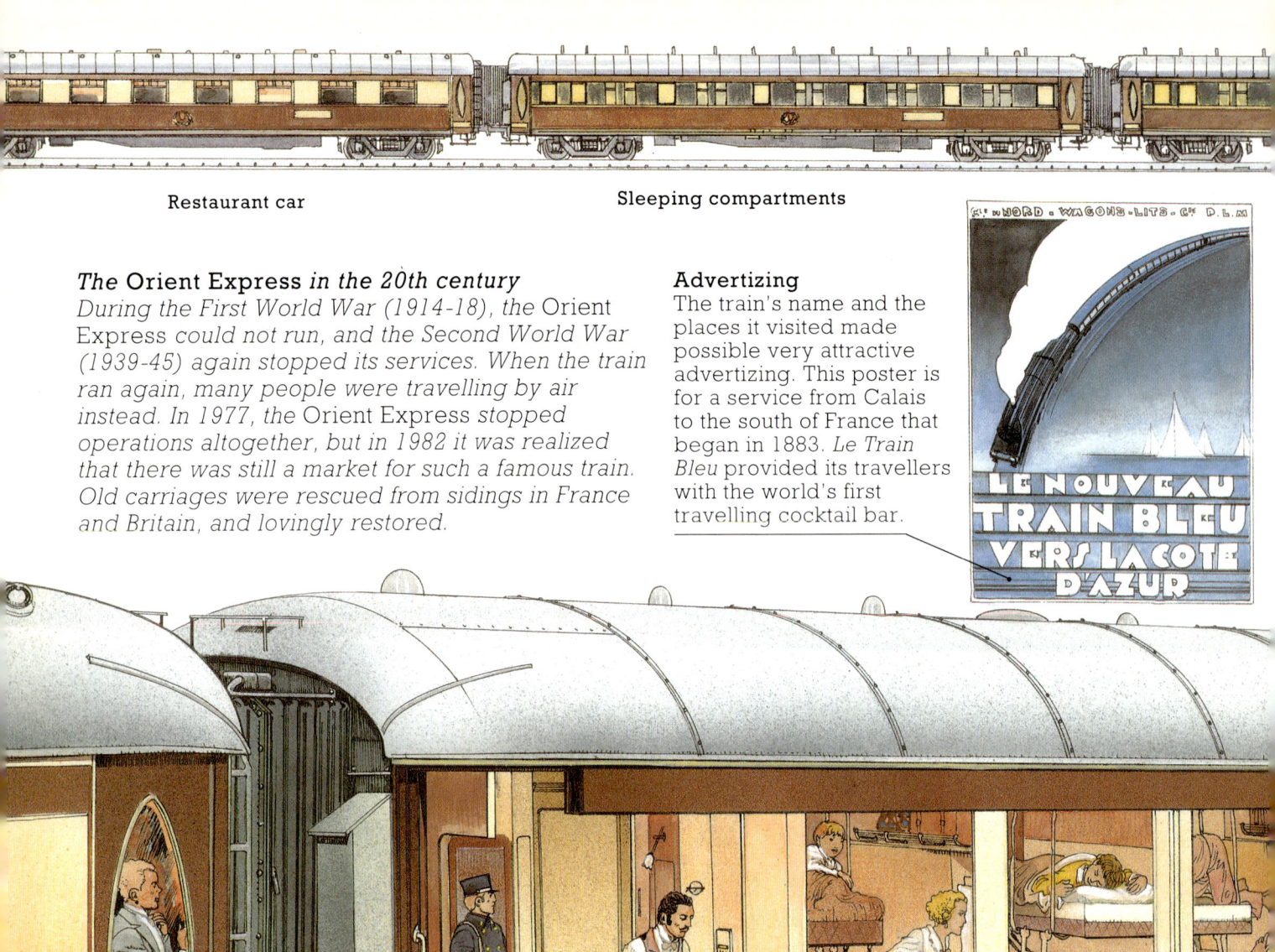

Restaurant car   Sleeping compartments

The Orient Express *in the 20th century*
During the First World War (1914-18), the Orient Express could not run, and the Second World War (1939-45) again stopped its services. When the train ran again, many people were travelling by air instead. In 1977, the Orient Express stopped operations altogether, but in 1982 it was realized that there was still a market for such a famous train. Old carriages were rescued from sidings in France and Britain, and lovingly restored.

Advertizing
The train's name and the places it visited made possible very attractive advertizing. This poster is for a service from Calais to the south of France that began in 1883. *Le Train Bleu* provided its travellers with the world's first travelling cocktail bar.

Ticket collectors wore a distinctive blue uniform

Comforts of home
The early carriages had a toilet cabinet with marble fittings. Later, a fully-equipped bathroom was added, containing towels embroidered with the *Orient Express* logo.

At night
Nagelmackers divided his coaches into sleeping compartments in which there were two beds covered in silk sheets, woollen blankets and eiderdowns. Each compartment had a bell to call the attendant.

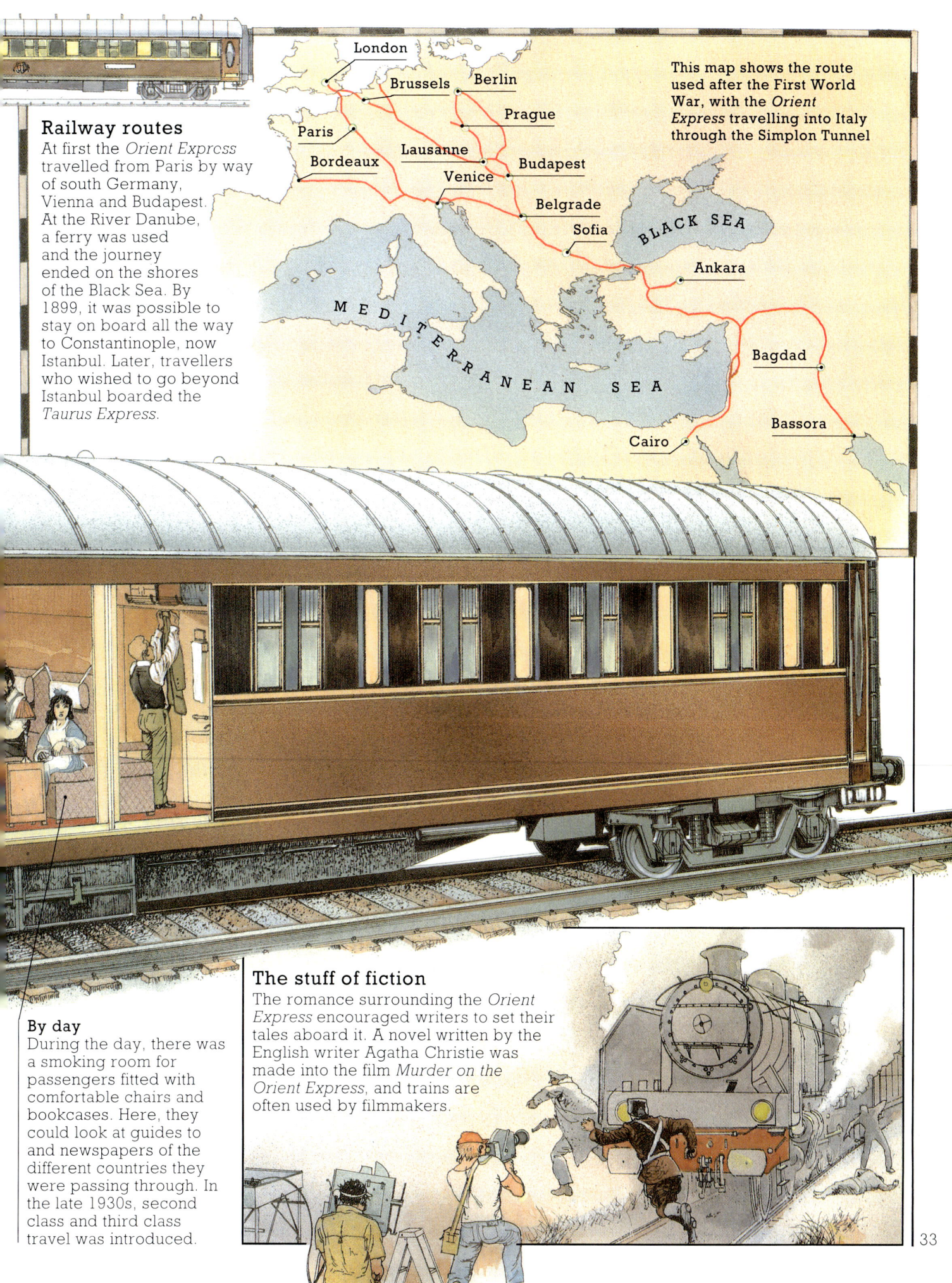

Railway routes

At first the *Orient Express* travelled from Paris by way of south Germany, Vienna and Budapest. At the River Danube, a ferry was used and the journey ended on the shores of the Black Sea. By 1899, it was possible to stay on board all the way to Constantinople, now Istanbul. Later, travellers who wished to go beyond Istanbul boarded the *Taurus Express*.

This map shows the route used after the First World War, with the *Orient Express* travelling into Italy through the Simplon Tunnel

By day

During the day, there was a smoking room for passengers fitted with comfortable chairs and bookcases. Here, they could look at guides to and newspapers of the different countries they were passing through. In the late 1930s, second class and third class travel was introduced.

The stuff of fiction

The romance surrounding the *Orient Express* encouraged writers to set their tales aboard it. A novel written by the English writer Agatha Christie was made into the film *Murder on the Orient Express*, and trains are often used by filmmakers.

A POWER RACE

Steam locomotives are costly to maintain and needed huge quantities of coal. They usually have to stop to pick up water, and the smoke that pours from their chimneys spatters people with soot and stains buildings. For many years, inventors searched for other sources of power to pull trains. They found the answers to the problems of steam in diesel engines and electric motors.

End of an era
Diesel and electric locomotives first appeared in the 19th century, and by the 1930s were becoming very popular. By the 1940s and 1950s, steam power was being replaced on a massive scale. The J 4-8-4 below was built for the Norfolk and Western Railroad in the United States. The last steam locomotive for that line was built in 1953.

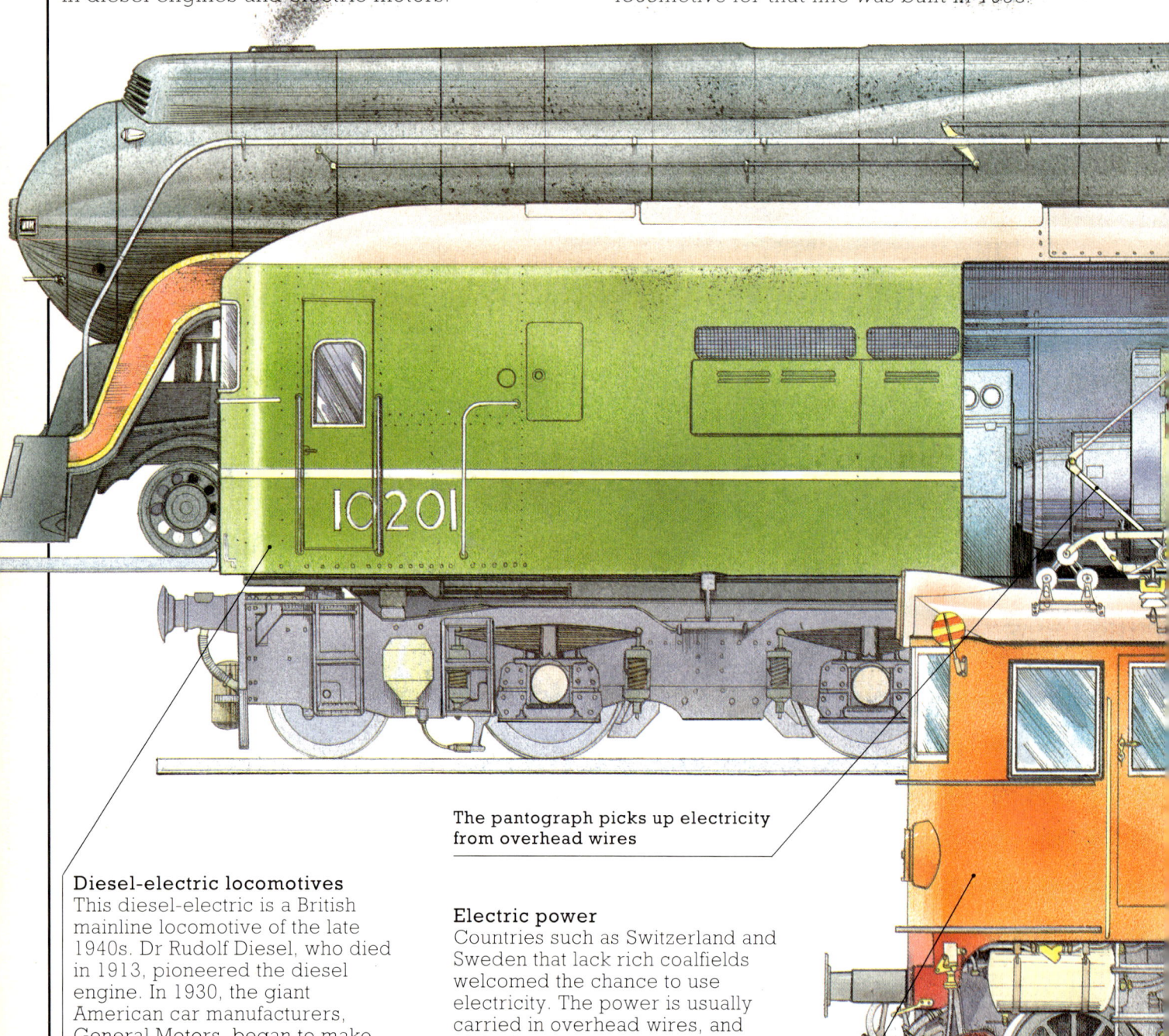

Diesel-electric locomotives
This diesel-electric is a British mainline locomotive of the late 1940s. Dr Rudolf Diesel, who died in 1913, pioneered the diesel engine. In 1930, the giant American car manufacturers, General Motors, began to make large numbers of reliable diesel units. The diesel engine powers an electric generator. This generator then supplies electric traction motors that in turn power the axles. The engines are costly to build, but more efficient to run than steam engines.

The pantograph picks up electricity from overhead wires

Electric power
Countries such as Switzerland and Sweden that lack rich coalfields welcomed the chance to use electricity. The power is usually carried in overhead wires, and picked up by engines like this one used on Swedish Railways in the 1940s. Sometimes, power is carried on a third rail. It is expensive to supply the lines that carry the current. But electricity provides a cleaner, more reliable and more powerful form of transport.

The leading wheels guide and support the engine

Wheels within wheels

Steam locomotives are identified by numbers. The first number refers to the "leading wheels" that guide and support the engine. The second number describes the main wheels or "driving wheels". The third number accounts for the "trailing wheels" at the rear of the locomotive. Diesel and electric engines are described by the number of their axles, instead of their wheels.

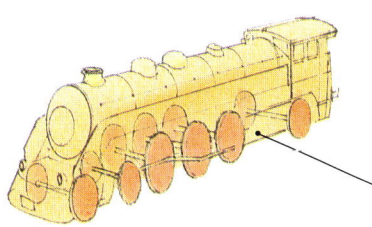

The Pacific 4-6-2, developed by the English engineer Alfred de Glehn, was the first Pacific class to run in Europe

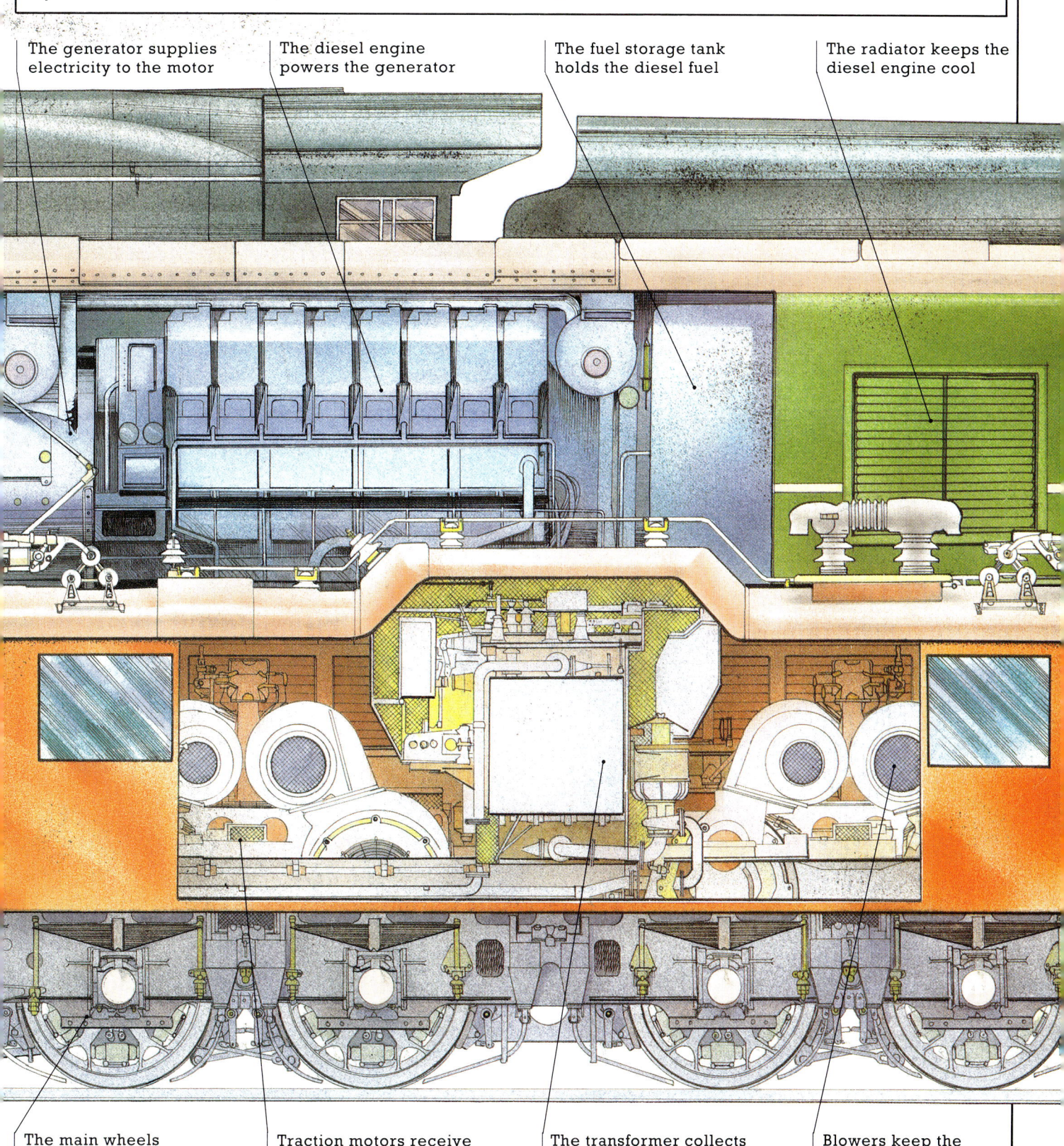

The generator supplies electricity to the motor

The diesel engine powers the generator

The fuel storage tank holds the diesel fuel

The radiator keeps the diesel engine cool

The main wheels are the driving wheels

Traction motors receive power from the transformer

The transformer collects current from the pantograph

Blowers keep the traction motor cool

35

LAST GASP

Steam locomotives could only hold their own against diesel and electric trains if engineers could find ways to make trains go faster. The Swiss inventor Anatole Mallet worked at increasing the power produced by the engine. In 1876, Mallet invented the "compound engine". Instead of going straight to the blastpipe and chimney, steam leaving the cylinder passed first to a low pressure cylinder, so providing further power. In 1891, the German engineer, Wilhelm Schmidt, devised the "superheater". An arrangement of pipes led the steam through a chamber containing hot gases from the firebox, so increasing the temperature. When Mallet's and Schmidt's ideas were brought together, they led to the building of the most efficient steam expresses ever seen.

Racing along
In 1893, Locomotive 999 had managed a speed of 180kph (112mph), on New York Central's line. By May 1936, a German steam locomotive hauling a train on the Berlin-Hamburg line reached 199.2kph (over 124mph). Railway companies in every country competed with one another to provide the fastest trains, trying to attract travellers to steam travel by offering the excitement of speed.

The *Flying Scotsman*
One of the most famous locomotives in the world, the *Flying Scotsman* was designed by Sir Nigel Gresley for the LNER, and is still brought out to impress audiences today. From 1928, it provided a world record non-stop service over the 632km (392 miles) between London and Edinburgh. The *Flying Scotsman* scooped up water from troughs in the track as it rushed along so that it would not have to stop.

The *Mallard*
The lines of the London and North Eastern Railway (LNER) lay up the eastern side of Britain and its chief engineer was Sir Nigel Gresley. In the 1930s, he decided that if he fitted streamlined casing over his locomotives it would increase their speed. In 1938, the *Mallard*, one of these new high speed engines, reached a speed of 203kph (126mph) while pulling a seven-coach train down a gradient. This has remained the world record for steam-hauled trains.

The *Hiawatha*

This famous American train was specially built to provide high speed passenger travel across the United States. The service began in 1935 on the Chicago, Milwaukee, St Paul and Pacific Line. The 660km (409 miles) from Chicago to St Paul was covered in just 5 hours 5 minutes. The train's average speed was 131.5kph (82mph), though it did manage a top speed of 168kph (105mph).

Big Boy

Big Boys were the largest, heaviest and most powerful steam locomotives in the world. Built for the Union Pacific Railroad in the United States, they first appeared in 1941. Each locomotive weighed 350 tonnes and carried with it 95,466 litres (21,000 gallons) of water. *Big Boys* were based on the ideas of Anatole Mallet.

Garrett engines

The Englishman Herbert William Garrett was an engineer who tried to make bigger locomotives. A giant-sized engine was too heavy for the track and had difficulty cornering. In 1907, Garrett produced a single boiler placed between two engine units, with water on one and fuel on the other. This spread the weight and allowed the engine to travel round sharp curves.

UP FRONT

In 1908, Henry Ford produced a cheap reliable car - the "Model T" - that he made in great numbers. This marked the start of a new transport revolution. Cars, lorries and buses began to pour off the production lines of factories in Europe and North America. They provided door to door travel that was more convenient than going by train. By 1917 there were nearly five million cars in the United States and the American government began an extensive road-building programme for the extra vehicles to use. In Europe, too, new roads were built including an early motorway system in Germany. At the same time, railway companies faced another threat - air travel had developed into a reliable and fast service.

At first, the railway companies replied by

The driver sits in a cab right on top of the *Settebello*

The American *Zephyr*
On 26 May 1934, the Burlington Railroad Company's new diesel-powered train *Pioneer Zephyr* made a record-breaking run. The *Zephyr* hurtled over the route between Chicago and Denver so rapidly it covered the distance in just over 13 hours - half the time of previous records! This success marked the arrival of long-distance "streamliner" services in the United States. The rival Union Pacific introduced its own version, the M.1000.

The Italian *Settebello*
Imagine travelling on a train that looks like an airliner! This was the exciting possibility that Italian State Railways offered to travellers from 1953. Its *Settebello* service hurtled up and down the line that linked Milan to Rome. The driver sat in a kind of cockpit above the passenger coach so that passengers could enjoy clear views forwards and backwards along the route. This popular and luxurious service was part of the TEE service.

providing more luxurious travel. In the 1930s, the increasing use of diesel and electric locomotives helped them to run cleaner and more reliable services. After the Second World War (1939-45), railway companies found it harder to compete and turned to their governments for help. In the United States, Amtrak was set up with government help to run diesel and electric locomotives.

High speed efficiency
Powerful, streamlined diesel-powered locomotives began to appear in North America and Europe. In 1957, a network linking Europe's main cities, the Trans-European Express, was set up. The TEE service covers nine different countries, with 35 trains operating 27 different routes. High speed luxury passenger services became popular worldwide.

The TEE coaches are made from stainless steel

Amtrak Metroliners averaged more than 144kph (90mph)

The *Rheingold*
In 1928, the German *Rheingold* was one of Europe's great express services. Since 1965 this train has become part of the TEE network. Whereas once it was hauled by steam locomotives, then by diesels, now it is powered by electricity. Its journey begins in Amsterdam and continues through Holland across Germany and into Austria. Its passengers travel in great comfort in sound-proofed coaches made of stainless steel.

Amtrak
In the United States there are enormous distances to cover, long trains to be pulled, and steep climbs through the Rocky Mountains. This all means that powerful locomotives are needed. In 1971, the organization Amtrak was set up with money from the government to provide a high speed passenger service from city to city. Amtrak ran the new United Aircraft Turbotrains, which were diesel, as well as the electric Metroliners.

THE TRAIN NOW STANDING...

The India Railway Board controls lines that make up the biggest railway network in Asia and the fourth biggest in the world. There are 60,320km (37,700 miles) of track which include main lines built to a broad gauge of 1,981mm (5ft 6in), local lines built to a metre gauge, and narrow gauge lines as well. Indian railways are very popular, with over ten million people travelling on them each day. To serve these passengers, the railway has more than 7,000 stations. Some are just simple wooden platforms and huts, but vast and splendid buildings serve the cities. One of the biggest of all, Howrah Station, was built in 1906 in Calcutta. The Victoria Terminus at Bombay is certainly one of the grandest stations in the world. It is decorated with domes, stained glass windows and sculptures.

A meeting place
Indian railway stations are very important centres of local and national life. Huge numbers of people gather in them to wait for trains, to meet friends and family, or to buy and sell all sorts of things. The larger stations include restaurants and waiting-rooms, where passengers with tickets may sit or stretch out and sleep.

Ticket offices
Because the railways are so popular, ticket offices in India often have very long queues. It is not unusual for Indian travellers to arrive many hours in advance of their train - sometimes even days early - and sleep in the station. But second class travel in India is one of the cheapest in the world.

Class division

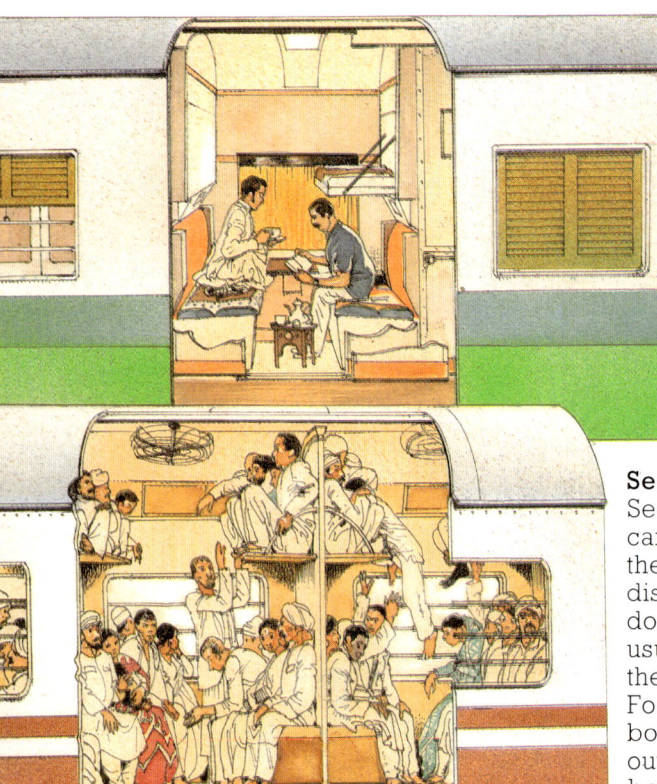

First class travel
Indian passenger trains are divided into classes. The faster main line trains include first-class compartments with two or four berths. Many of these carriages are air-conditioned and some have private showers and toilets. Only wealthy Indians and tourists can afford to travel in such comfort and eat in the restaurant cars.

Second class travel
Second class compartments carry far more people than the first class ones. On long distance trains the seats fold down into bunks. Passengers usually bring bedding, though they can hire it in the station. Food can be bought from boys who run up and down outside the carriages before the train leaves.

Shops
In stations across the world, travellers will find book and newspaper shops, restaurants and shops selling snacks. These places help to pass the time not only for those on the trains, but also for passengers waiting in the station.

Timetables
The huge Indian railway network is complicated to organize. The system is divided into seven separate zones, each with its own timetable. Travellers ask the station porters to help them find their trains.

A hive of activity
For some people, stations are places where they spend most of their lives. While some people sleep, others bustle about trying to sell goods. Since Hindu beliefs include a special respect for cows, these animals may wander in to stations looking for food.

On the track
Electric or diesel locomotives pull main line express and mail trains. However, steam engines are still used to pull some of the trains that run on the slow local lines. These trains are a feature of local life. When there is no room for goods inside the train, they often carry them on the roofs of the goods wagons.

EN ROUTE

The first railway passengers had to be tough. Third class passengers travelled in open wagons with holes drilled in the floor so that downpours of rain could drain away. But railway companies soon learned that taking proper care of passengers meant far more people would travel on their trains. In 1863, George Mortimer Pullman built a coach called the *Pioneer* that was very comfortable to travel in. However, it cost four times as much as other coaches, and railway companies did not buy Pullman's coaches until two years later in 1865.

Candles and oil lamps lit up early coaches. In 1850, an American company introduced gas lighting and by 1885 the first electric lights were in use. Seating improved too, though early travellers on Japanese railways who were used to sitting on rush matting found the padded seats unusual. Heating also improved. Early passengers shivered, but in 1881 steam heating was introduced in American carriages.

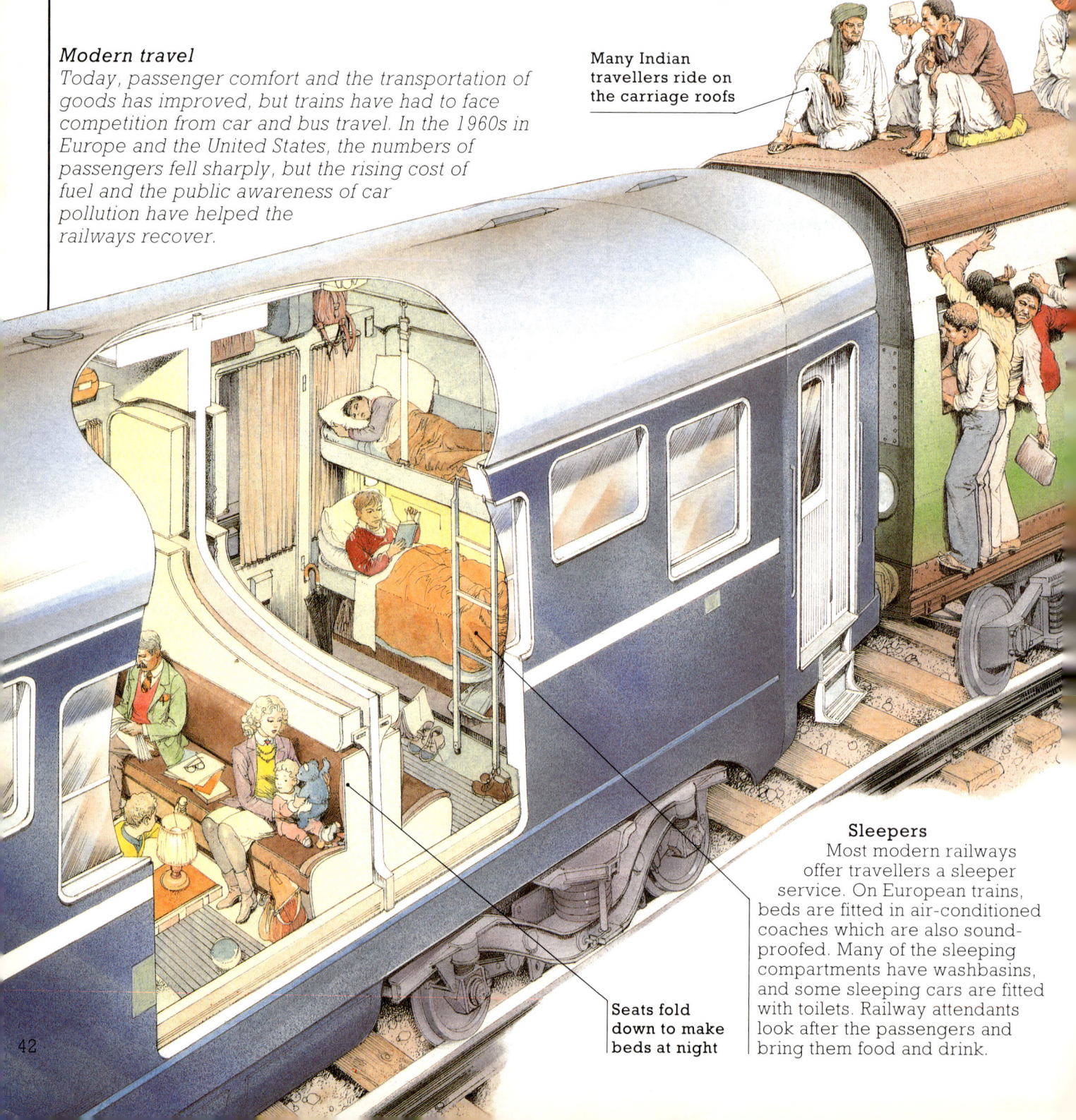

Modern travel
Today, passenger comfort and the transportation of goods has improved, but trains have had to face competition from car and bus travel. In the 1960s in Europe and the United States, the numbers of passengers fell sharply, but the rising cost of fuel and the public awareness of car pollution have helped the railways recover.

Many Indian travellers ride on the carriage roofs

Seats fold down to make beds at night

Sleepers
Most modern railways offer travellers a sleeper service. On European trains, beds are fitted in air-conditioned coaches which are also soundproofed. Many of the sleeping compartments have washbasins, and some sleeping cars are fitted with toilets. Railway attendants look after the passengers and bring them food and drink.

Travel through India
Steam trains are still common in India, and travelling by train in India is not expensive. The railways are very popular and passengers crowd onto the trains as best they can, particularly on short journeys. Some people try to travel without paying by jumping onto the carriages as the train sets off. These travellers have to hang onto the windows and handrails. The wind and rain, the heat of the burning sun and clouds of dust mean that their journeys are often very dangerous.

Wheels on wheels
Over the centuries, many different kinds of railway wagon have been designed to transport all shapes and sizes of freight. Car-transporters are used by some car-makers to send their vehicles out to the salerooms. Such transport forms a large part of the railway freight business in places such as the United States. The transporters are also widely used by people who want to take their cars with them on holiday, but do not want the long, tiring drive to their destination.

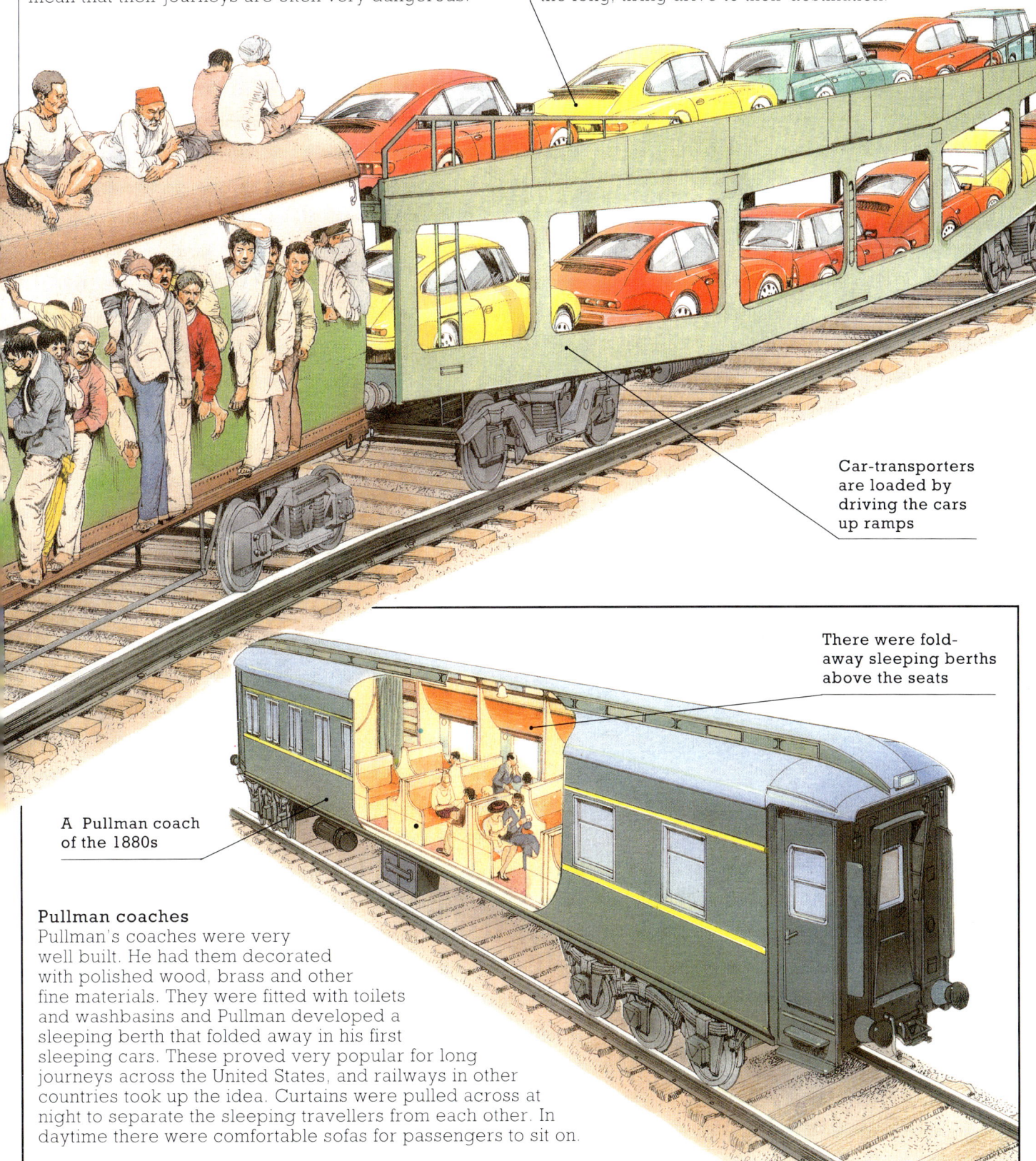

Car-transporters are loaded by driving the cars up ramps

There were fold-away sleeping berths above the seats

A Pullman coach of the 1880s

Pullman coaches
Pullman's coaches were very well built. He had them decorated with polished wood, brass and other fine materials. They were fitted with toilets and washbasins and Pullman developed a sleeping berth that folded away in his first sleeping cars. These proved very popular for long journeys across the United States, and railways in other countries took up the idea. Curtains were pulled across at night to separate the sleeping travellers from each other. In daytime there were comfortable sofas for passengers to sit on.

A variety of uses
Modern railway companies have to think of new ways of attracting customers. For the passenger, this can mean more comfortable carriages or different ways of passing the journey time. For the freight companies, the main interest is in a faster, more efficient service.

The "vista dome", invented by the Canadian, T. J. McBride, is built above the main body of the carriage

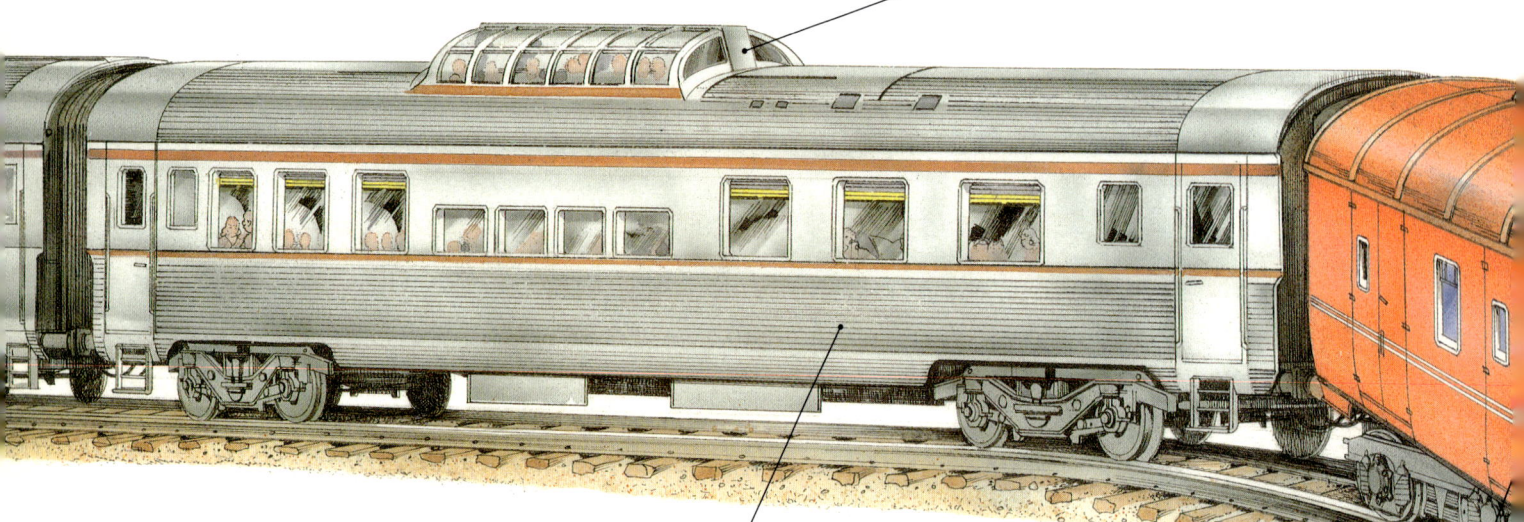

A clear view
Many railways travel through beautiful scenery and one of the pleasures of travel is the opportunity to admire the landscape through which the train is travelling. Some trains are designed with observation cars to give passengers an uninterrupted view. In 1902, the Canadian Pacific Railway introduced carriages fitted with special viewing areas called "vista domes".

Sorting it out
Cheap and fast letter and parcel delivery became possible when, in 1838, the first travelling post office ran along a railway. Soon the post was being sorted by workers in specially-made carriages. But attacks by robbers and the growth of very large sorting offices led to this method of sorting becoming less common.

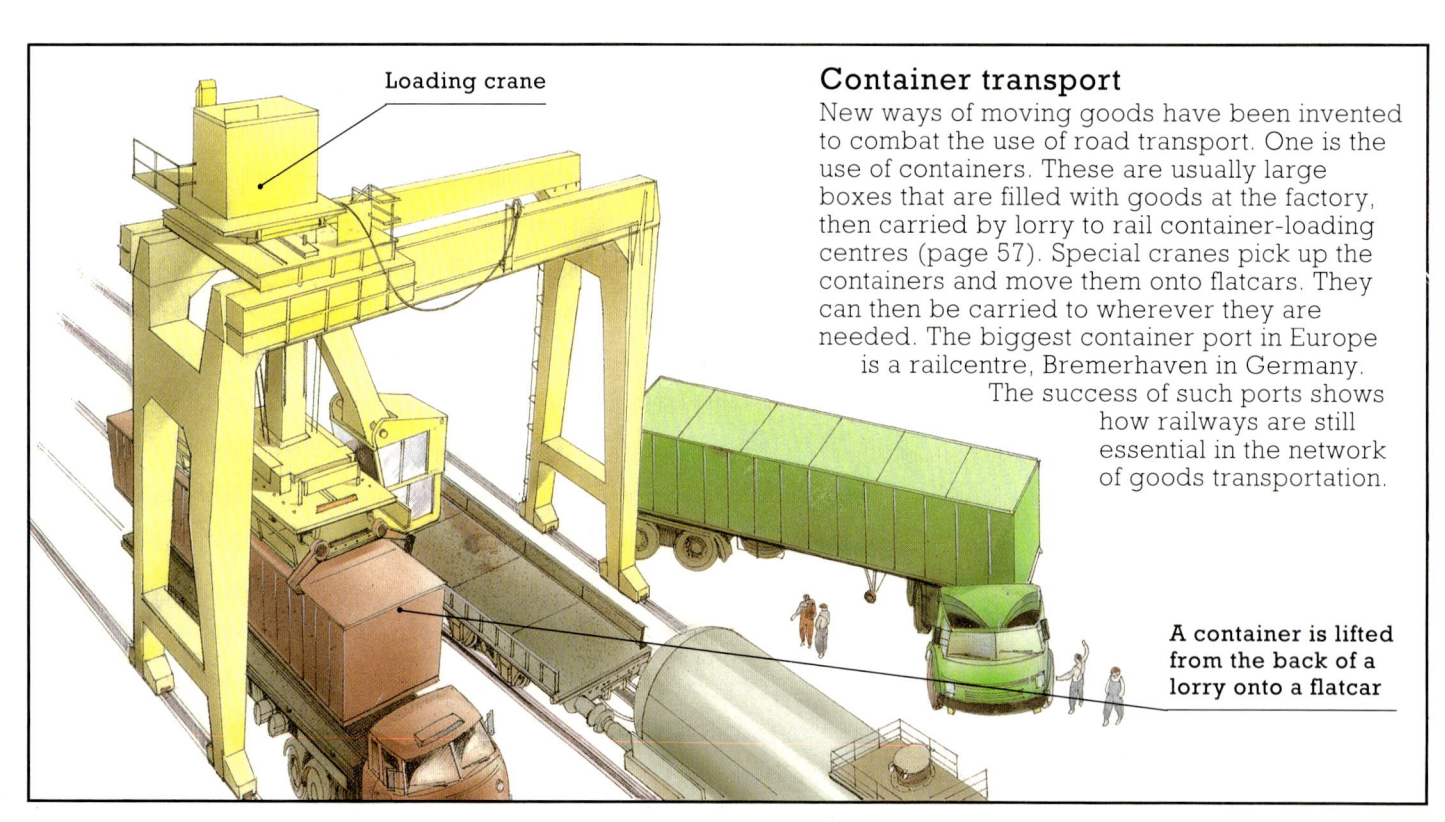

Loading crane

Container transport
New ways of moving goods have been invented to combat the use of road transport. One is the use of containers. These are usually large boxes that are filled with goods at the factory, then carried by lorry to rail container-loading centres (page 57). Special cranes pick up the containers and move them onto flatcars. They can then be carried to wherever they are needed. The biggest container port in Europe is a railcentre, Bremerhaven in Germany. The success of such ports shows how railways are still essential in the network of goods transportation.

A container is lifted from the back of a lorry onto a flatcar

Catching the post
In the early days of the railway, the mail was loaded onto trains only when the train was in a station. Then came an invention that did away with these stops. The mail was placed in bags and hung on hooks alongside the track. As the trains went speeding past, they used special nets to catch up the mail bags and drop off sorted mail for local distribution.

The mail-vans of the travelling post offices (TPOs) are attached to fast passenger trains

The way forward?
French railways have made great efforts to attract customers. Their SNCF network can provide many different kinds of coaches that can be ordered for special events. These include a disco-car that has a dance floor, a bar, special loud-speakers and lighting, and a lounge area. Customers can also hire a cinema that seats sixty people and a coach designed as a conference room.

CITY TRAVEL

Until the second half of the 19th century, Japan had kept itself separate from the rest of the world. Then the Japanese began to trade with other countries. This led to the development of industries, including shipbuilding and the manufacture of steel. In 1872, a railway line opened between Tokyo and Yokohama. By 1880 most cities in Japan were linked by rail.

During the 20th century, the population of Japan has grown in size. Because almost three-quarters of the country is mountainous, and much of it is covered in forest, expanding towns and cities have had to crowd into coastal areas. On the main island of Honshu, especially, a long narrow strip that includes cities like Tokyo and Osaka, houses most of the population. A first-class travel network is essential to the country.

A teeming population

About 123 million people live in Japan, and three quarters of them are city dwellers. One district of Tokyo, Shinjuku, contains one of the world's busiest stations. Nine different railway and underground lines come together there, and more than two million people pass through the station every day.

Underground

There are underground railway systems in most of Japan's major cities, such as Tokyo and Osaka. Tokyo's lines were begun in the 1920s and form an extensive system. Few parts of the city are more than five minutes from a subway station. The underground is heavily used, about five million people crowding onto it every day. During rush hours, the system employs broad-shouldered officials in uniforms and white gloves whose job it is to push as many people as possible onto the trains.

Changing track

Today, there is an extensive programme of track-laying in Japan to widen the many narrow gauge lines to carry modern trains. The very mountainous landscape had caused the original engineers to recommend a narrow gauge of 1,066mm (3ft 6in).

The rail network

During the 20th century, Japan Railways has developed under the control of the government. Today, it has about 21,091km (13,106 miles) of 1,066mm (3ft 6in) track, about a quarter of which has been electrified. Recently, it has been split up into seven companies, and is increasingly run by private groups.

Chinese railways

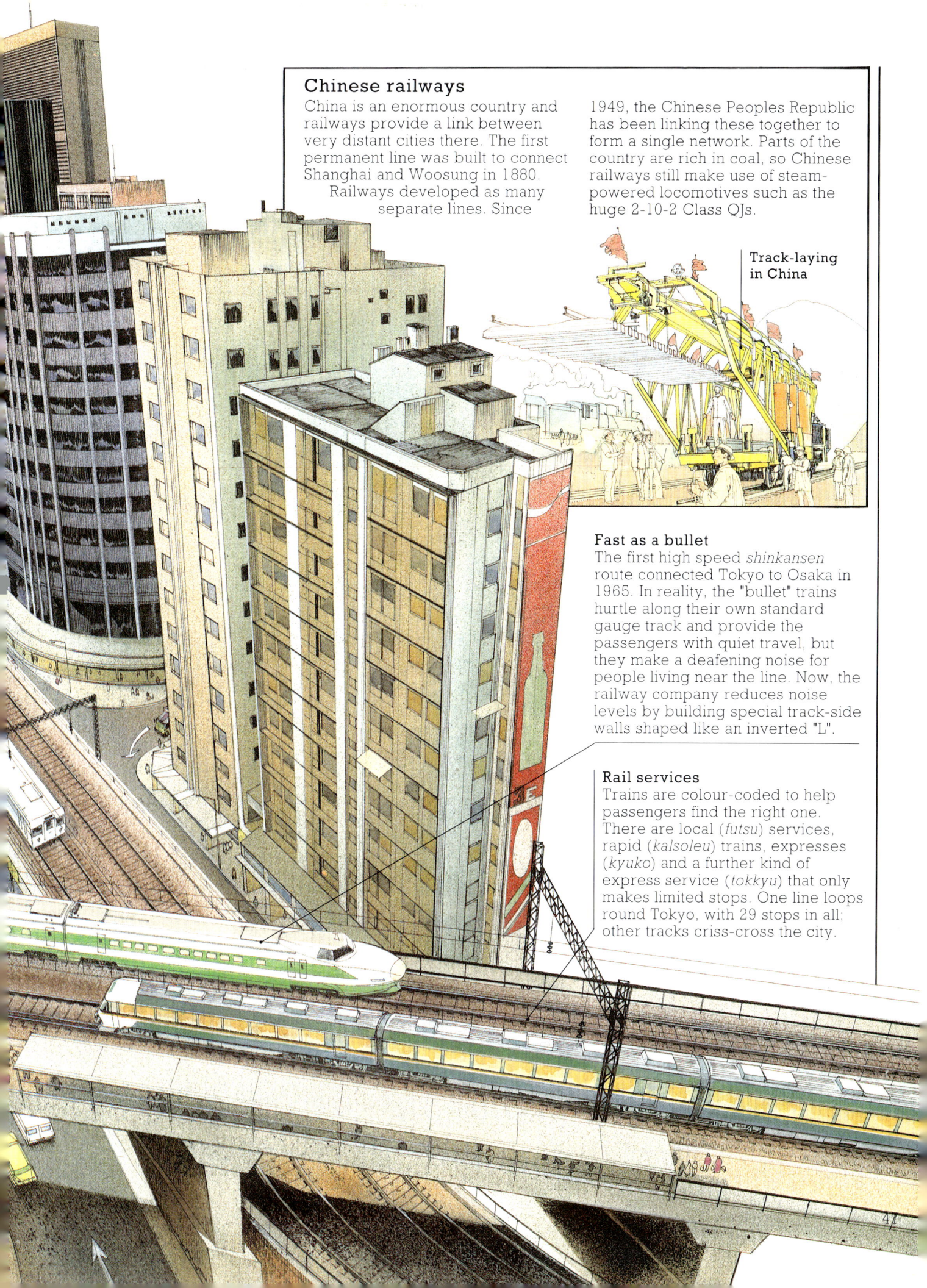

China is an enormous country and railways provide a link between very distant cities there. The first permanent line was built to connect Shanghai and Woosung in 1880. Railways developed as many separate lines. Since 1949, the Chinese Peoples Republic has been linking these together to form a single network. Parts of the country are rich in coal, so Chinese railways still make use of steam-powered locomotives such as the huge 2-10-2 Class QJs.

Track-laying in China

Fast as a bullet

The first high speed *shinkansen* route connected Tokyo to Osaka in 1965. In reality, the "bullet" trains hurtle along their own standard gauge track and provide the passengers with quiet travel, but they make a deafening noise for people living near the line. Now, the railway company reduces noise levels by building special track-side walls shaped like an inverted "L".

Rail services

Trains are colour-coded to help passengers find the right one. There are local (*futsu*) services, rapid (*kalsoleu*) trains, expresses (*kyuko*) and a further kind of express service (*tokkyu*) that only makes limited stops. One line loops round Tokyo, with 29 stops in all; other tracks criss-cross the city.

GOING UNDERGROUND

As cities grew, their buildings spread out over more and more land. Cities became so huge that walking to work, to the shops and to entertainments became increasingly difficult in streets crowded with horse-drawn vehicles.

Engineers realized that the answer lay in underground railways. In 1863, the first such line opened in London. In 1900, the Paris Metro and the New York subway opened, and many other cities around the world followed suit. The development of cars, motor buses and lorries slowed down building during the early 1900s, but today interest in underground railways has revived. Motor traffic brings noise, pollution, traffic jams, and the destruction of buildings to create roads and car parks. Underground trains can carry more people without causing this damage.

An expanding network
Between 1960 and 1990, about 12 new underground lines were built every five years. Today, 35 cities are building, or planning to build, new lines. These works include a huge project to construct 163km (101 miles) in Beijing, China. Trains have to be carefully controlled because so many rush at high speed through the tunnels.

Travel by "tube"
The "cut and fill" method of construction (see below) is only possible near the surface. In 1870, the first "tube" was opened. The track ran inside a metal tube beneath London's River Thames. Today, lines are dug at all sorts of depths.

The first underground
In London in 1863, the Metropolitan and District Railway opened the first underground in the world. It was made by digging a deep trench in the street, supporting the trench sides with walls and making a roof of brick arches and iron girders. The street was then replaced. This method is called "cut and fill". The engineer in charge, John Fowler, used a steam locomotive called *Fowler's Ghost* to pull carriages.

Ticket office

New lines in a system can be placed in "tubes" that pass above or below older lines

Better safe than sorry
At first, some people were scared that there would be accidents, while others worried about fire on the underground or that they would not be able to breathe properly. Companies installed ventilator shafts and fans, alarms on trains and, more recently, closed-circuit television.

Ventilator shaft

Through the ages
Steam engines clearly produced too much smoke for long underground lines. The first electric line opened in London in 1890 and by 1905 most undergrounds were using electricity. Power was picked up from a third rail running along the track.

Going down?
In 1911, the first moving staircase, or escalator, came into service at Earls Court Station, London, England At first, people did not trust it, so the railway paid a man with a wooden leg to ride up and down to prove its safety! The longest escalator in the world today is at Leningrad Station, Russia. It rises 59.5m (195ft).

The City and South London Railway, which opened in 1890, ran through cast iron tubes, and carried little electric locomotives pulling carriages with high, tiny windows

1897

By the beginning of the 20th century, the engine and the driver's cab had been engineered so that they had become part of the front carriage

1907

Getting on
At rush hour, passengers pour on and off trains in huge numbers. For example, the new line in Hong Kong has eight-car trains, each of which can carry 3,300 people. Because of this enormous influx of people, stations have to be planned so that people can move in and out quickly, buying tickets from machines, following clear maps and passing through automatic gates.

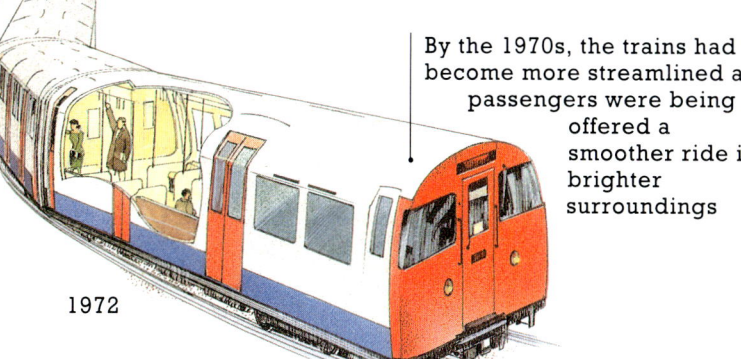

By the 1970s, the trains had become more streamlined and passengers were being offered a smoother ride in brighter surroundings

1972

A condensing steam locomotive cut down the amount of steam

TUNNELS AND TUNNELLING

Long stretches of the world's railways lie inside tunnels. Tunnels can be made in a number of ways. Those close to the surface are often built by "cut and fill" - digging a deep trench, building walls and roofing, then filling in the trench (pages 48-49). Deeper tunnels cannot be created like this. They have to be bored or hacked out from rock and clay well below the surface. Where a tunnel is to be laid on the bed of a large river or under the sea, a level trench is sometimes dredged out, and sections of tubing lowered from barges into the trench. Divers fasten the sections together, and seal the joints. A tunnel made like this carries trains 40m (130ft) below the surface of San Francisco Bay in the United States. Tunnels through mountains are usually built in the way shown in this scene.

Deep underground
The many stages of work shown here would, in reality, be spread across a considerable distance. The building methods used are known as "drill and blast". Hard rock is shifted by blowing it to pieces with explosives placed in drill holes. The workers are using the "bench" method in which the top half of the tunnel is finished first.

Safety first
Tunnelling has always been dangerous. Modern workers wear hard hats to protect themselves from injury. Yet rock and earth falls can bury them, and water may burst in and sweep them away. The workers also need a supply of fresh air. This comes from ventilation shafts drilled down into the tunnel, and from air pumped along.

Early tunnelling
The men who built the first railway tunnels hacked at rock with picks and blew it up with gunpowder. The machine shown here marked a big step forward. It was designed by the Italian, Germains Sommeiller, to cut the Fréjus tunnel 12km (5 miles) through a mountain to link French and Italian railway lines. He developed a drill powered by compressed air, and fitted several of these drills to a wheeled carriage.

Moving materials
The rock and earth that has been dug away is called "spoil". It is continuously cleared away or "mucked out" as tunnelling proceeds. Special machines often fitted with sound-proofed cabs do this work.

Drilling and blasting
Machines like these are called "jumbos". They are really a modern development of Sommeiller's invention. A jumbo is fitted with several drills, each of which is mounted on a moveable arm. The drills bore holes that are usually about 3m (10ft) deep into the hard rock. Explosive charges are then placed inside the holes.

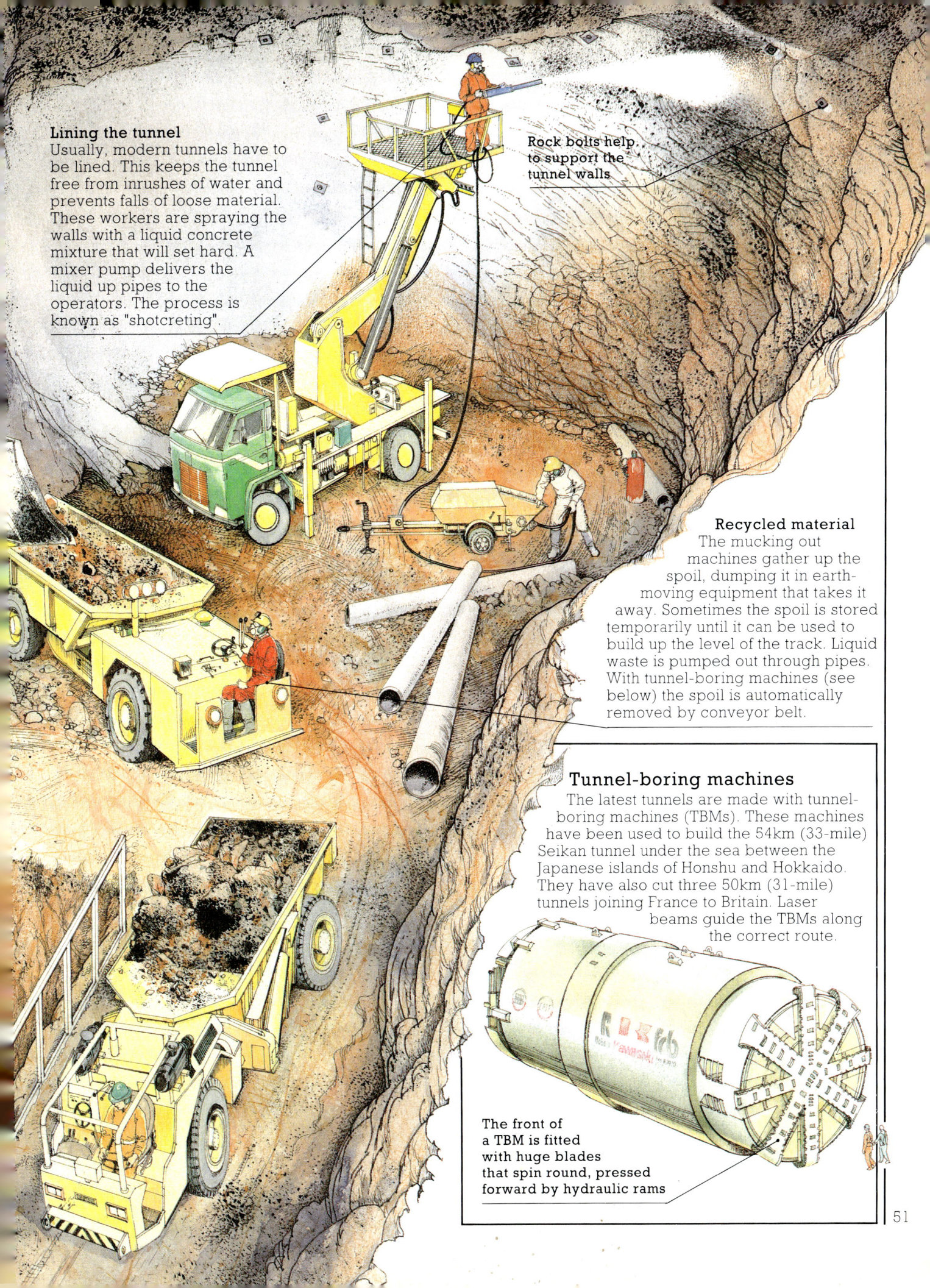

Lining the tunnel
Usually, modern tunnels have to be lined. This keeps the tunnel free from inrushes of water and prevents falls of loose material. These workers are spraying the walls with a liquid concrete mixture that will set hard. A mixer pump delivers the liquid up pipes to the operators. The process is known as "shotcreting".

Rock bolts help to support the tunnel walls

Recycled material
The mucking out machines gather up the spoil, dumping it in earth-moving equipment that takes it away. Sometimes the spoil is stored temporarily until it can be used to build up the level of the track. Liquid waste is pumped out through pipes. With tunnel-boring machines (see below) the spoil is automatically removed by conveyor belt.

Tunnel-boring machines
The latest tunnels are made with tunnel-boring machines (TBMs). These machines have been used to build the 54km (33-mile) Seikan tunnel under the sea between the Japanese islands of Honshu and Hokkaido. They have also cut three 50km (31-mile) tunnels joining France to Britain. Laser beams guide the TBMs along the correct route.

The front of a TBM is fitted with huge blades that spin round, pressed forward by hydraulic rams

51

OVERCOMING OBSTACLES

The land that railways have to cross is sometimes too hilly and steep to be shaped for track simply by cutting away rock and earth. Where railways cross rivers and estuaries, the building problems are sometimes very difficult and complicated to solve. When George Stephenson (page 8) built the line from Manchester to Liverpool in 1830, he had to construct as many as 63 bridges, as well as a viaduct to carry track over a canal. During the last 150 years, different building techniques have been developed to cross different obstacles. For example, the methods used to build a bridge over a deep, narrow gorge are very different from those used to built a viaduct over a wide valley.

Up and over
Sometimes, railway builders deliberately choose to build lines up very steep mountains because passengers are attracted by the view and by the excitement of the journey. These pages show some of the ingenious ways in which railway engineers have overcome the greatest obstacles.

The "rack" railway
In 1889, the world's steepest "rack" railway opened. It runs up Mount Pilatus in Switzerland, on a system designed by Edward Locher. The rack is a long centre rail with teeth on either side that are gripped firmly by the train, preventing it from slipping backwards.

Pushing on
The engines that power the Pilatus line are very powerful and push the trains up the steep gradients. The early locomotives were steam-powered, but from 1937, electric engines have been used. The passengers travel in carriages that are specially designed to fit the angle of the slope.

52

Bridges
Early bridge builders had to use simple methods and tools, and basic materials. But modern machinery and the use of better building materials have led to the development of a great variety of designs.

Viaduct - a many arched span needed to cross a lengthy area of low land

Arch - a strong single span, made from stone, brick, concrete or metal

Trestle - a bridge supported by trestles which are networks of wood or metal

Girder - steel girder sections that meet at, and rest, on strong stone or brick pillars

Cantilever - balanced and linked bridge sections resting on strong supports

Narrow gauge lines
Narrow gauge lines twist and turn up and down mountains where the slopes do not need rack or cable. This is the Rhaetian Railway in Switzerland which opened in 1889. It carries people to popular winter skiing resorts. Here, it is crossing the Landwasser Viaduct, which is 65m (213ft) high.

Funiculars
Ordinary railways cannot make very steep climbs, but cable or funicular railways can. There are usually two tracks with a carriage on each. The cables are wound round stationary engines at each end and the weight of one carriage being lowered is used to pull the other one up the slope.

Avalanche!
Heavy snowfalls in mountainous areas can loosen snow and cause avalanches. Railway lines are often protected by concrete roofing, which allows the snow to sweep harmlessly over the track. In the United States, the Santa Fe's *El Capitan* passes through shelters like these.

53

Building bridges
On 28 December 1878, part of a huge bridge across the River Tay in Scotland collapsed. The crew of a train and 73 passengers died. This disaster was a terrible warning to engineers: future bridges must be built properly, and checked and repaired regularly.

Trestle bridges
There are many trestle bridges in the United States. The early railway builders used the plentiful supplies of timber and the trestle design suited this material. During the Civil War, bridge builders like Herman Haupt became skilful at replacing damaged trestle bridges quickly.

Maintaining and repairing
Heavy trains hurtling along at speed shake track loose. Storms, floods and landslides can also damage the line. Early track repair kept great numbers of workers busy. Today, modern machines like this one automatically check, lift, level ballast and re-fasten lines.

Arch bridges
On an arch bridge, the arch can be above or below the track. In the case of the world's largest steel-span arch bridge, stretching 503m (1,650ft) over Sydney Harbour, Australia, it is above it. The Pfaffenberg Zwenberg Bridge in Austria is the longest concrete-span arch bridge, at 200m (660ft).

Cantilever bridges
The longest cantilever span in the world is the Quebec Bridge in Canada. It opened in 1917 and carries the track of the Canadian National Railway over the St Lawrence River. The most famous is the Forth Bridge near Edinburgh in Scotland. This was built by 4,500 workers and took seven years to complete.

The Forth Bridge is 2,529m (8,298ft) long and crosses the Firth of Forth at a height of 47.5m (156ft)

Girder bridges
Girder bridges are usually used to span narrow gaps, but sections can be linked to each other. When properly designed and made, they are very strong. For this reason, after the collapse of the Tay Bridge, the new designer, W.H. Barlow, decided to use a series of girder bridges.

Sturdy upright pillars support the metal girders that carry the track

55

MOVING GOODS

Railway companies earn most of their money by carrying goods from place to place. In some countries, such as Russia, this side of rail transport is vital. However, moving goods from factories to customers, from ports to inland destinations, is a complicated business to organize. All over the world, railways have built special areas called "marshalling yards" where goods are sorted out. Maschen yard near Hamburg in Germany is probably the most modern marshalling yard in Europe. In a single day, it can handle 120 southbound trains as well as 150 going north. There are 306km (190 miles) of track packed into 283 hectares (690 acres) at Maschen. Yet very few people operate the yard, because computers do most of the work.

A modern marshalling yard
Marshalling yards must be efficient. Journey times have to be speedy and trains must be organized as quickly as possible. It is also essential that the right goods reach the right destination. Marshalling yards are usually divided into two sections. In one, wagons gather as they enter the yard. In the other, long trains bound for the same destination are put together.

A signal box
Both in marshalling yards and on the main line, accidents must be avoided and trains switched by points onto the correct routes. The first signalmen did this work in signal boxes. They moved levers that controlled wires that in turn worked the signal arms and the points on the line. Messages were sent from station to station by means of electric bells and by Morse Code signals tapped out on telegraph lines. By the 1890s, signals and points were connected and could be operated together.

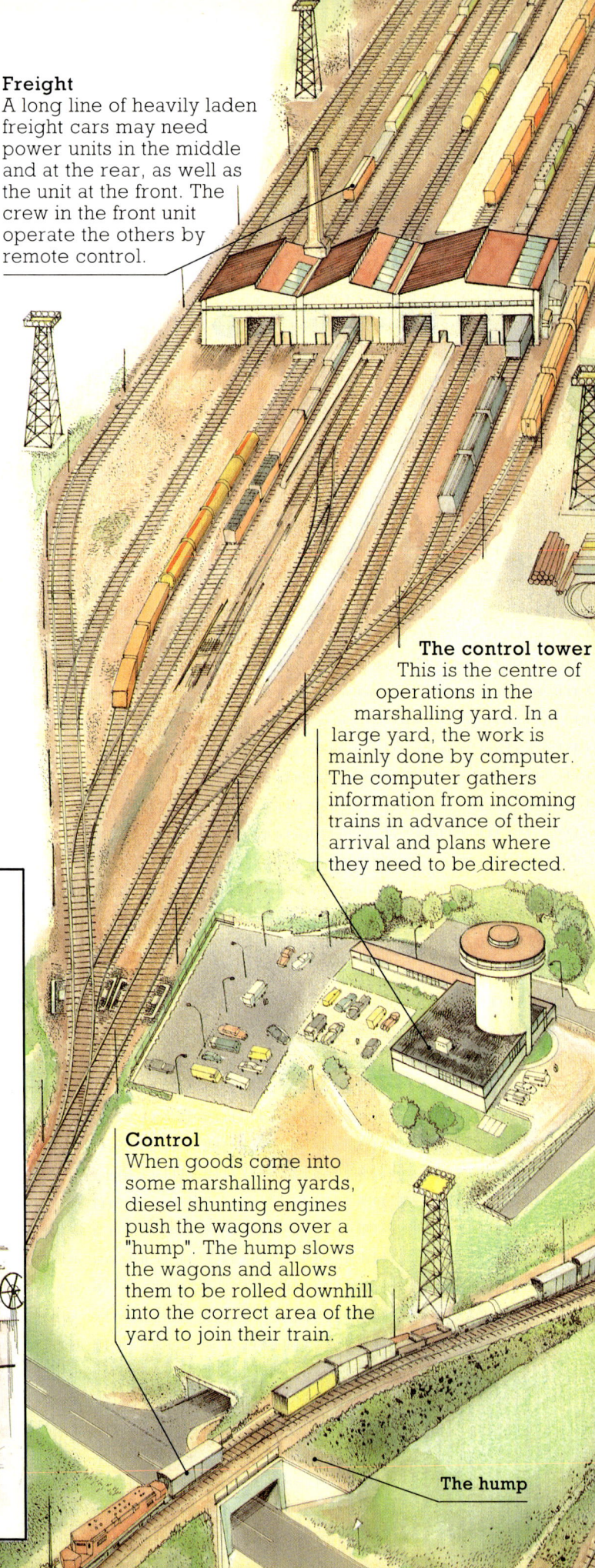

Freight
A long line of heavily laden freight cars may need power units in the middle and at the rear, as well as the unit at the front. The crew in the front unit operate the others by remote control.

The control tower
This is the centre of operations in the marshalling yard. In a large yard, the work is mainly done by computer. The computer gathers information from incoming trains in advance of their arrival and plans where they need to be directed.

Control
When goods come into some marshalling yards, diesel shunting engines push the wagons over a "hump". The hump slows the wagons and allows them to be rolled downhill into the correct area of the yard to join their train.

The hump

Signalling

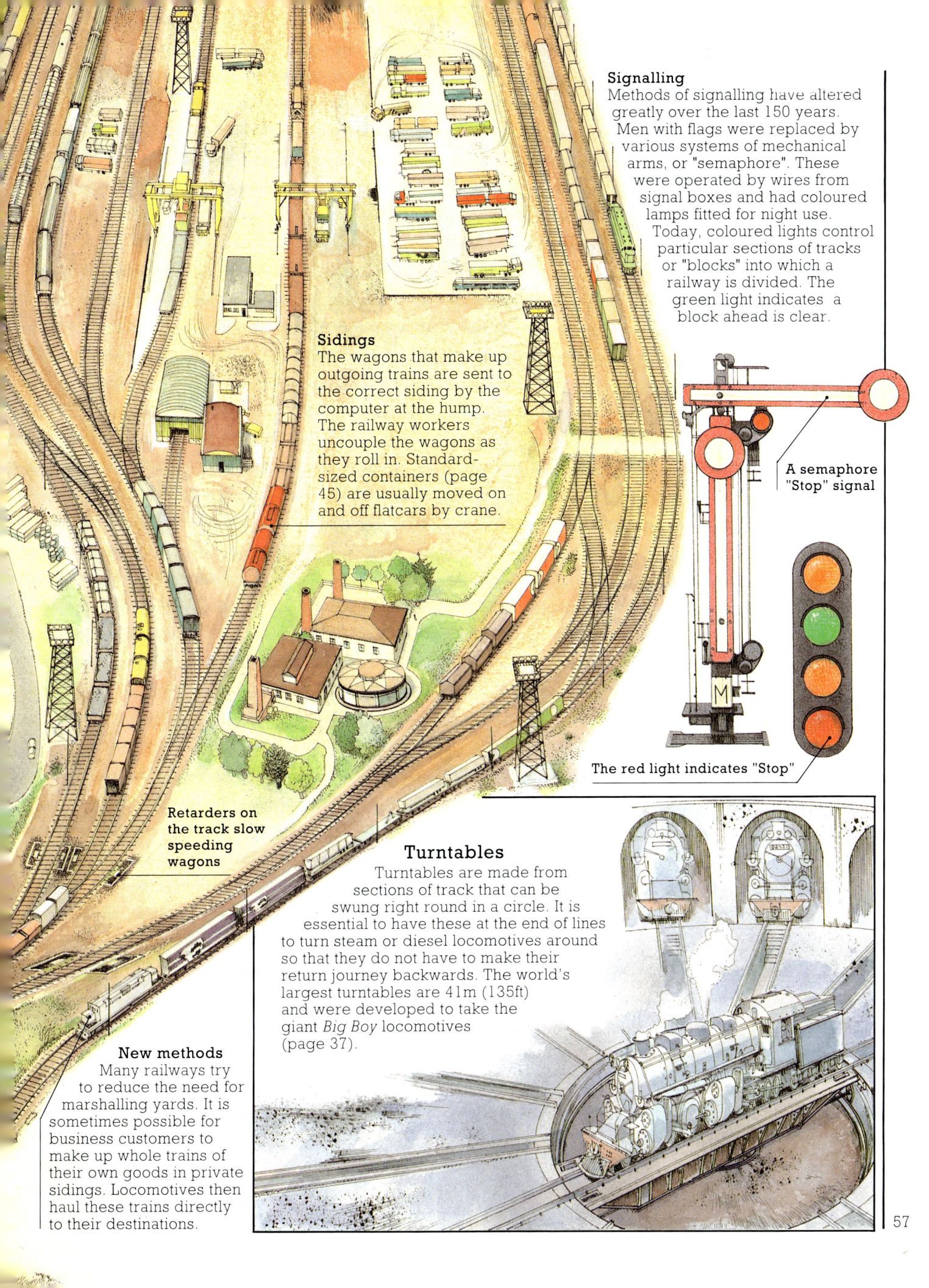

Methods of signalling have altered greatly over the last 150 years. Men with flags were replaced by various systems of mechanical arms, or "semaphore". These were operated by wires from signal boxes and had coloured lamps fitted for night use. Today, coloured lights control particular sections of tracks or "blocks" into which a railway is divided. The green light indicates a block ahead is clear.

A semaphore "Stop" signal

The red light indicates "Stop"

Sidings

The wagons that make up outgoing trains are sent to the correct siding by the computer at the hump. The railway workers uncouple the wagons as they roll in. Standard-sized containers (page 45) are usually moved on and off flatcars by crane.

Retarders on the track slow speeding wagons

Turntables

Turntables are made from sections of track that can be swung right round in a circle. It is essential to have these at the end of lines to turn steam or diesel locomotives around so that they do not have to make their return journey backwards. The world's largest turntables are 41m (135ft) and were developed to take the giant *Big Boy* locomotives (page 37).

New methods

Many railways try to reduce the need for marshalling yards. It is sometimes possible for business customers to make up whole trains of their own goods in private sidings. Locomotives then haul these trains directly to their destinations.

RIDING THE RAILS

Railways are used to attract your attention. Famous engines decorate postage stamps; railway scenes from the past are often used in film and television programmes. Composers have even written pieces of music inspired by railways.

Some people are so enthusiastic about railways that they are prepared to give up their spare time to repair and rebuild old railway engines. One of the most unusual of these "trains for fun" takes its passengers back into the times of the old west in North Carolina, USA, with men dressed up as bandits carrying out raids on the trains. Many countries now have huge railway museums such as the German Museum at Mulhouse, and the Indian Rail Transport Museum in New Delhi.

Going for a ride
People "ride the rails" in all sorts of places and often for no other reason than the simple pleasure of the trip. In fairgrounds and theme parks all over the world, tracks twist and turn, climb and dip, rush through water, and even loop the loop.

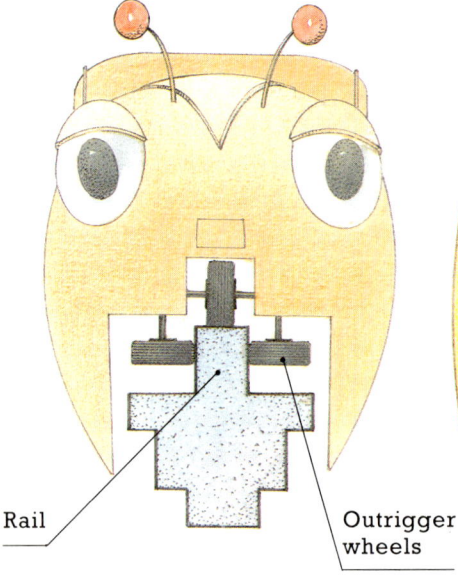

Early days
In 1810, the first monorail that we know about opened to carry food for troops in London, England. It was built with wooden boards nailed to posts, and horses pulled the cars. In 1876, General Roy Stone built the first monorail to carry passengers, across Fairmont Park, Philadelphia, in the United States.

Rail

Outrigger wheels

Monorails
The ladybird train is running on a single rail or "monorail". There are different sorts of monorail; this one follows what is called the "Alweg" system. On either side of the rail is a narrow roadway. The train has wheels that run on the rail, and balancing "outrigger" wheels. There is an Alweg monorail in India, the Patiala Railway, that is 96km (60 miles) long.

The outrigger wheels run along the roadway on each side of the rail and hold the train steady

In miniature
Steam locomotives made such an impact that toy-makers began making models of them in tin and wood. Early steam-driven engines left trails of water behind and are therefore usually called "dribblers". Clockwork motors were used too. The German firm of Marklin led the way in developing standard engines like "O" and "1". In 1920, Frank Hornby began to produce train sets that rivalled the fine ranges made by Marklin.

Today, making and running model railways is a very popular hobby

Other monorails
The Alweg system is one of three main types. The Lartigue method balances the train over the rail as on the Irish Line (page 29). The "Langen" type is still in use in Germany, taking people over the River Wupper in cars that hang below a single rail.

Record breakers
Which is the world's smallest public railway? There are a number of contenders for the title. This is the Romney, Hythe and Dymchurch line in south-east England. It opened in 1927 and runs on 380mm (15in) gauge track. The line from Wells Harbour in England, has track only 260mm (10in) wide.

AT TOP SPEED

People have always enjoyed going as fast as possible by whatever type of transport is available. Business executives like to spend as little time travelling as possible. Modern motorways and air services are threats to passenger rail travel, but many of the world's railways have replied to their rivals by providing very fast, quiet and comfortable trains. In 1991 in Germany, for example, a new service of high speed gleaming white trains began a service between the cities of Hamburg and Munich at speeds that reach 282kph (175mph). Like most new high speed sources this one is powered by electricity. "Pantographs" link the overhead power line to the locomotive.

Staying on the rails
High speed trains need special track. When Japanese Railways developed their high speed trains, they laid standard gauge track. When the trains joined 1066mm (3ft 6in) track a third rail had to be added.

Pantograph

125s in Australia
Railways have played a very important part in the development of Australia. They join together the widely separated cities. This XPT service is based on the High Speed 125 diesel-electric locomotives used by British Rail. Like the British version, each 125 has two power cars fitted with twelve cylinder turbo-charged diesel engines. Services running at up to 160kph (100mph) link the cities of Sydney and Melbourne.

Controlling trains at top speed

The faster trains speed along, the harder it is for the driver to see the ordinary line-side signals. Very fast trains also take time to slow up and stop. This means, for example, that there are no level crossings on the lines travelled by Japan's bullet trains. Today, the electronics revolution has transformed the problem of controlling high speed expresses. Computers are used in many countries to gather, organize and send out information. They automatically plan the journeys of trains, detect changes that need to be made, and pass on instructions. This is a control centre on the high speed Paris to Lyons route in France. A small number of people control a complicated system by keeping in radio contact with the train drivers.

The bullet train
Japan's bullet train pioneered very high speed services as early as 1965. Gleaming, aerodynamically designed trains hurtled along a route between Tokyo and Osaka at speeds up to 210kph (131mph). This *shinkansen* route (page 47) proved enormously popular - on one day in 1975 it carried over 800,000 passengers. By May 1976, more than 1,000 million people had travelled on it.

The TGV
In 1981, SNCF (the French National Railways) launched their new high speed service of "Trains à Grande Vitesse" (TGV). A special new track had been laid from Paris to Lyons. Along it rushed an express train that reached a new world record speed of 380kph (238mph)! Its average speed cut the journey time between the two cities by almost half. The train's very powerful disc brakes bring it to a halt in 3.1km (1.86 miles).

DOWN THE LINE

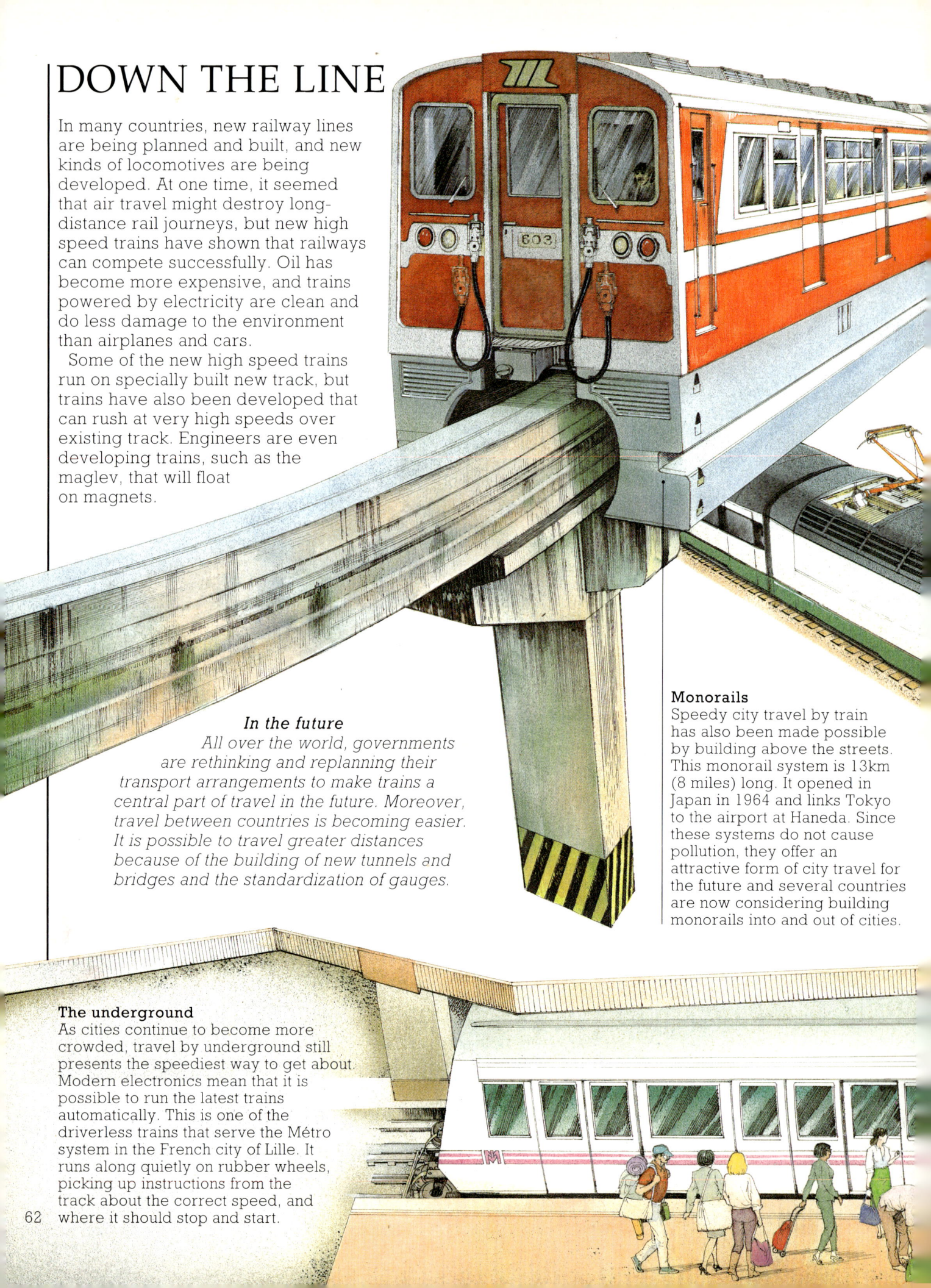

In many countries, new railway lines are being planned and built, and new kinds of locomotives are being developed. At one time, it seemed that air travel might destroy long-distance rail journeys, but new high speed trains have shown that railways can compete successfully. Oil has become more expensive, and trains powered by electricity are clean and do less damage to the environment than airplanes and cars.

Some of the new high speed trains run on specially built new track, but trains have also been developed that can rush at very high speeds over existing track. Engineers are even developing trains, such as the maglev, that will float on magnets.

In the future
All over the world, governments are rethinking and replanning their transport arrangements to make trains a central part of travel in the future. Moreover, travel between countries is becoming easier. It is possible to travel greater distances because of the building of new tunnels and bridges and the standardization of gauges.

Monorails
Speedy city travel by train has also been made possible by building above the streets. This monorail system is 13km (8 miles) long. It opened in Japan in 1964 and links Tokyo to the airport at Haneda. Since these systems do not cause pollution, they offer an attractive form of city travel for the future and several countries are now considering building monorails into and out of cities.

The underground
As cities continue to become more crowded, travel by underground still presents the speediest way to get about. Modern electronics mean that it is possible to run the latest trains automatically. This is one of the driverless trains that serve the Métro system in the French city of Lille. It runs along quietly on rubber wheels, picking up instructions from the track about the correct speed, and where it should stop and start.

Tilting trains

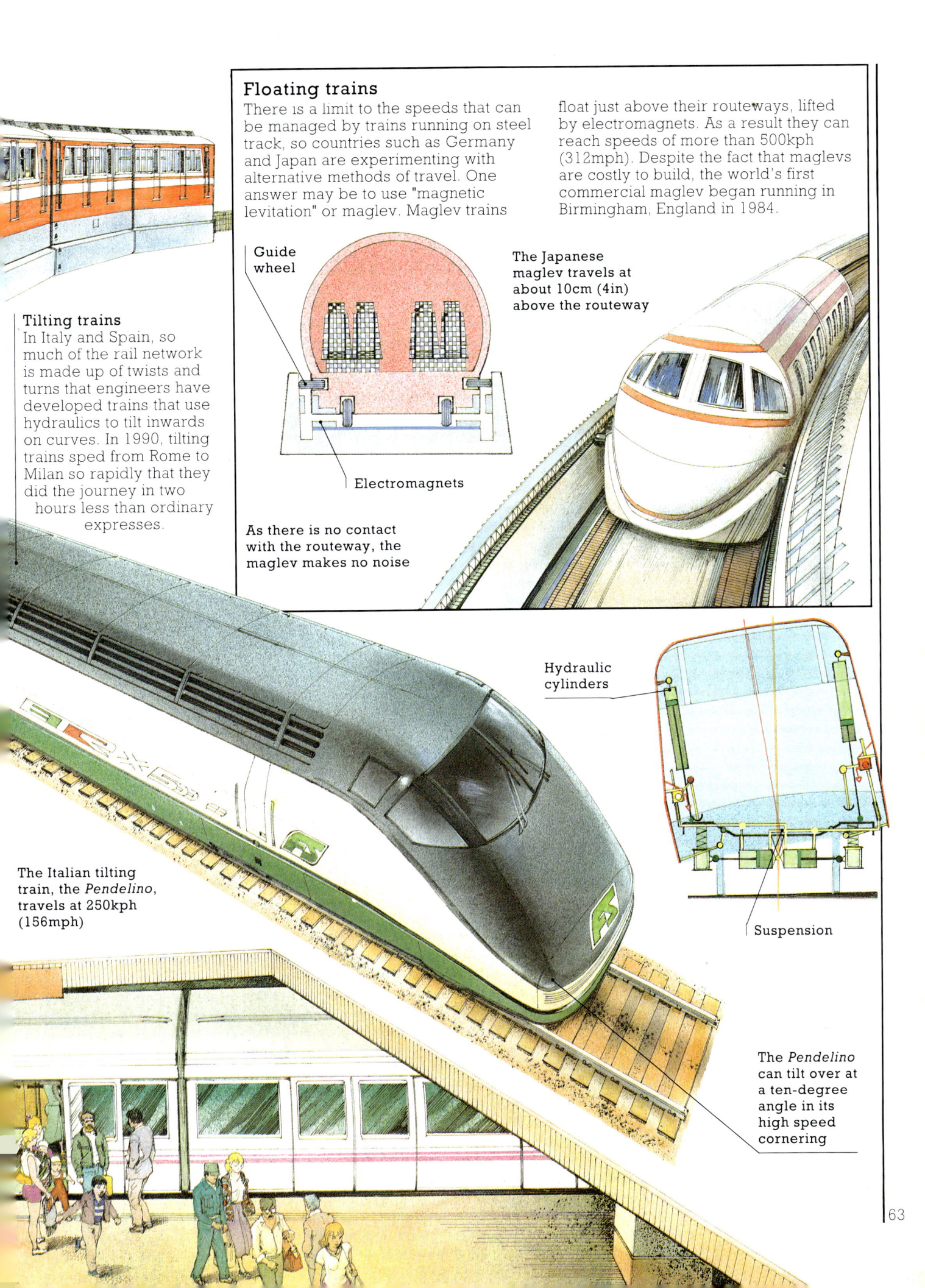

In Italy and Spain, so much of the rail network is made up of twists and turns that engineers have developed trains that use hydraulics to tilt inwards on curves. In 1990, tilting trains sped from Rome to Milan so rapidly that they did the journey in two hours less than ordinary expresses.

Floating trains

There is a limit to the speeds that can be managed by trains running on steel track, so countries such as Germany and Japan are experimenting with alternative methods of travel. One answer may be to use "magnetic levitation" or maglev. Maglev trains float just above their routeways, lifted by electromagnets. As a result they can reach speeds of more than 500kph (312mph). Despite the fact that maglevs are costly to build, the world's first commercial maglev began running in Birmingham, England in 1984.

Guide wheel

The Japanese maglev travels at about 10cm (4in) above the routeway

Electromagnets

As there is no contact with the routeway, the maglev makes no noise

The Italian tilting train, the *Pendelino*, travels at 250kph (156mph)

Hydraulic cylinders

Suspension

The *Pendelino* can tilt over at a ten-degree angle in its high speed cornering

INDEX

Amtrak 39
Astley, Philip 24
avalanche shelters 53
axles 34, 35

Bailey, George F. 24
Baltimore and Ohio Railroad 28
Barlow, W.H. 55
Barnum, Phineas Taylor 24
Big Boys 37, 57
Birkenshaw, John 9
boilers 8, 20, 29, 37
box relays 18
Braithwaite, John 9
Brassey, Thomas 10
bridges
  archway 53, 54
  cantilever 53, 55
  girder 53, 55
  trestle 53, 54
  viaducts 10, 53
Brunel, Isambard Kingdom 12, 26, 27
Brunton, William 28
building
  railways 4, 10-11, 16-17, 27, 50-51, 52-53
  stations 4
  underground 48
bunkhouse cars 16
Burlington Railroad Company 38
Burstall, Timothy 9
"Butch" Cassidy 19

cable railways 53
Canadian Pacific (CP) Railroad 39, 44
carriages 4, 7, 23, 25, 52
  steam 6
  underground 49
car-transporters 43
Catch Me Who Can 7
Central Pacific Railroad 17, 18, 20, 21
China, railways in 12, 47, 48
circus trains 24-25
coaches 7, 31, 39, 42, 43
Cody, Buffalo Bill 25
Compagnie Internationale des Wagons Lits 30
compartments 31, 32, 42, 43
container transport 44
Cook, Thomas 15
cowcatchers 20
Cugnot, Thomas 15
Custer, General 18
cylinders 20

Daddy Long Legs 28
de Glehn, Alfred 35
Diesel, Dr Rudolph 34

electric line, underground 49
electric locomotives 34, 39, 41, 52, 60
elevated railways 29
embankments 10

engines
  beam 7
  compound 36
  diesel 34, 35, 39, 41, 60
  steam 6, 7, 8, 20, 22, 28, 29, 34, 41, 52
Ericcson, John 9
escalators 49
express trains 22, 39

flatcars 25, 44, 57
Flying Scotsman 36
Forth Bridge 55
Fowler, John 48
Fowler's Ghost 48
freight trains 22, 43, 56-57
funicular railway 53

Garrett, Herbert William 37
gauge
  broad 12
  narrow 29, 46, 53, 59
  standard 12, 13, 39, 47, 60
Gooch, Daniel 12
goods, transport of 8, 14, 15, 26, 41, 43, 44, 56-57
Great Western Railway (GWR) 12
Gresley, Sir Nigel 36

Hackworth, Timothy 9
Haupt, Herman 54
Hedley, William 9
Hickok, James Butler ("Wild Bill") 21
high speed trains 36, 60, 62-63
Hornby, Frank 49
horse-drawn railways 8, 29
hump (driver's cab) 28
hump (marshalling yard) 56
Huskisson, William 9

immigrant trains 22
India, trains in 40-41, 42, 58
industries, growth of 26

James, Jesse and Frank 19
Japan, trains in 42, 46-47, 51, 60, 61, 62, 63
  bullet trains 47, 61
  shinkansen 47, 61
Jessop, William 8
Jupiter 17, 20-21

Kansas Pacific Line 17, 18

Lartigue, Charles 29, 59
Locher, Edward 52
Locomotion 8
Locomotive 119 17
locomotives 4, 6, 7, 8, 12, 16, 28, 31, 34, 35, 36, 37, 39, 41, 47
locomotive numbers 35
London and North Eastern Railway (LNER) 36
Losh, William 9

maglev 62, 63

Mallard 36
Mallet, Anatole 36, 37
marshalling yards 56
McBride, T.J. 44
mixed trains 22
model railways 59
monorails 58, 59, 62
  Alweg system 58, 59
  Langen system 59
mountain railways 28, 53, 54
  Pilatus, Mount 52
  Rhaetian Railway 53
Murdoch, William 6

Nagelmackers, Georges 30
Nasmyth, James 26
native Americans 16, 18, 23, 25
navvies 10, 11
Newcomen, Thomas 7
Norfolk and Western Railroad 34
Novelty 9

observation cars 44
Orient Express 30-31, 32-33
outlaws 18, 19

pantographs 34, 35, 60
passengers 7, 8, 22, 23, 40, 42, 43, 44
Perseverance 9
Pinkerton's National Detective Agency 19
Pioneer 42
Pioneer Zephyr 38
pistons 20
points 56
post office, travelling 44, 45
Promontory Point 17, 20
public railways
  first 8
  smallest 59
Puffing Billy 9
Pullman coaches 23, 43
Pullman, George Mortimer 23, 42

rack and pinion railways 28, 52
rails 6, 7, 8, 9, 11
railway workers 10-11, 27, 54
railways, first
  in Britain 7, 8, 9, 11
  in United States 14, 16-17, 18
Rainhill trials 9
restaurant cars 30
Rheingold 39
robberies 18, 19, 30, 44
Rocket 8, 9

Sanger, George 25
Sans Pareil 9
Schmidt, Wilhelm 36

Settebello 38
sidings 57
signalling 13, 56, 57, 61
  semaphore, use of 57
Sitting Bull 18
sleepers 9, 11
sleeping compartments 32, 42
SNCF (French National Railways) 45, 61
Sommeiller, Germains 50
Spalding, G.R. 25
spark arresters 20
station masters 14
stations
  main line 4, 5, 14, 15, 40-41, 46, 49
  underground 4, 46
steam engines 6, 7, 8, 20, 22, 28, 29, 34
steam excavators 11
steam hammer 26
steam power 6, 8-9, 20
Stephenson, George 8, 9, 12
Stephenson, Robert 8, 9
Stone, General Roy 58
"Sundance Kid", the 19
superheaters 36

Tay Bridge disaster 54, 55
telegraph 18, 56
third rail 34, 49
tilting trains 63
  Pendelino 63
timetables 14, 41
towns, growth of 16, 21, 26
track 4, 5, 7, 8, 9, 11, 28, 29, 46, 47, 60
Trains à Grande Vitesse (TGV) 61
tramways 6
Trans-European Express (TEE) 38, 39
Trevithick, Richard 6, 7
tunnel-boring machines (TBMs) 51
tunnelling 50-51
  "cut and fill" method 48, 50
  drill and blast method 50
tunnels 50-51
turntables 57

underground railways 4, 46, 48-49, 62
Union Pacific Railroad 16, 17, 21, 37, 38

vista domes 44
Volk, Magnus 28

Watt, James 6
Wells Fargo 19
wheels 9, 20, 28, 34, 35, 58

Acknowledgements
Dorling Kindersley would like to thank Janet Abbott, Lynn Bresler, Richard Czapnik, Marcus James and *Tunnels and Tunnelling* magazine for their help in producing this book.